BARTHOLOMEW
ILLUSTRATED REFERENCE
ATLAS
OF THE WORLD

*To Emma
from Granny 1986*

John Bartholomew & Son Ltd
Edinburgh

First published in Great Britain 1985 by
John Bartholomew & Son Limited,
12 Duncan Street, Edinburgh EH9 1TA
© John Bartholomew & Son Limited

British Library Cataloguing in Publication Data
The Bartholomew illustrated reference atlas of the world.
1. Atlases, British
912   G1021

ISBN 0-7028-0726-5

Acknowledgements
The Publishers acknowledge with thanks the assistance of the following in preparing this publication:
Dr Walter Stephen
Senior Adviser, Curriculum, Dean Education Centre, Edinburgh
Alister Hendrie
Assistant Headteacher, Portobello High School, Edinburgh
Andrew Grant
Principal Teacher, Geography, Wester Hailes Education Centre, Edinburgh
Stephen Hamilton
Principal Teacher, Geography, Broughton High School, Edinburgh

The Publishers are grateful to the following for providing the photographs used in this atlas:
(picture number(s) shown in italics)
Travel Photo International: pages 6-7, savanna, rain forest, prairie, northern forest; page 12, *7*;
page 21, *2*; page 27, *11*; page 28, *4, 5, 13, 14*; page 30, *7*; page 31, *2*; page 46, *3, 4*; page 54, *3, 4*
Photographers' Library: pages 6-7, scrub *Chris Knaggs photograph*, desert *Oliver Martel photograph*
page 10, *8 Clive Sawyer photograph*; page 26, *8 Ian Wright photograph*
page 29, *9 Tom Hustler photograph*; page 30, *4 Robyn Beeche photograph*
Biofotos page 10, *5 Heather Angel photograph*; page 30, *6 Andrew Henley photograph*
page 31, *3 Soames Summerhays photograph*
The Photo Source page 12, *10*; page 21, *4*; page 26, *7*
Wade Cooper Associates, Edinburgh page 28, *12*; page 29, *10*; page 46, *1*
Pictor International page 26, *6*; page 46, *2*
B. and C. Alexander pages 6-7, tundra
Bruce Coleman Ltd page 54, *6 WWF/Eugen Schuhmacher photograph*
Mepha page 21, *1 C. Osborne photograph*
Michael Scott pages 6-7, woodland and grass
Yorkshire and Humberside Tourist Board page 11, *2*

Printed in Italy by New Interlitho, Milan

CONTENTS

SCALE

This atlas for the 8-13 age group bridges the gap between pictorial atlases intended for young children and the much more complex atlases published for adults. The political and physical maps are just like those in a 'proper' atlas, drawn to scale with layer colouring to show how high the land is. But they have been simplified to make it easy to find country names, borders, main towns and physical features such as rivers and mountains. Where there is an English version of a place name, it is given first followed by the local language version.

The layout of the atlas is easy to follow. Pages 4 and 5 show how flat, two-dimensional maps can be drawn to show the rounded, three-dimensional world, and explain the idea of scale as it relates to maps. The map of world environments on pages 6 and 7 shows the 8 different climatic areas found in the world, with descriptions of the types of vegetation to be seen in each area. The key map and key to symbols on pages 8 and 9 will help in understanding and using the maps. Each of the boxes on the key map outlines an area covered by a particular map in the atlas. The number of the page where the map can be found is given in the inside top right-hand corner of each box. The symbols used on the maps are also explained, with examples.

The main part of the atlas, pages 10-58, is divided into continental sections – Europe, Africa, etc. Each section begins with a political map naming the countries included. Gazetteers for some of the larger countries show their flags and list their size, population, capital, language and currency. A 'Did you know that?' panel gives details of more unusual and surprising facts and places, some of which are illustrated. All the facts are keyed with numbers to their location on the political map. The number of each fact, the number of its picture (if there is one) and its number on the map are all the same. E.g. Fact ❹ is illustrated in picture ❹ and ❹ on the map shows where in the world it can be found. There are also maps showing population distribution, and the type of natural vegetation and products of each part of the continent. A location globe shows exactly where the area covered in the political map is, in relation to the rest of the world. Physical maps covering each part of the continent in more detail make up the rest of the continental section. On every map spread there is another location globe which provides a quick answer to the question 'Where in the world is that?'.

The last six pages of the atlas contain an index to many of the places and geographical features shown on the maps. Each entry gives the name of the place, what it is (island, region etc), the name of the country or part of the world where it can be found, and a page number and grid reference. So the entry: London *Eng* **16C3**, refers to London, England which can be found on the map on page 16, in the area located by running a finger down from the letter C at the top of the page and in from the number 3 at the side of the page.

Scale means how big one thing is, compared to another. For example, a model car can be a scale model of a real car. Drawing something 'to scale' is a way of making a picture or map of something big fit on to a small piece of paper. The important fact about a scale model or scale drawing is that from it, you can find out the size of the real thing – whether it is a car or a country. All you need to know is the scale that was used. The scale of a scale drawing will be shown on the scale bar beside it. It might look like this:

A short length (for example 1 cm) on the scale bar will stand for a longer one (for example 1 m) in the real world. By measuring the drawing and converting your measurements using the scale bar, you know the size of the real thing.

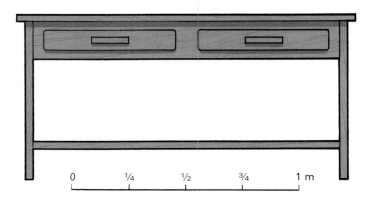

The picture shows a scale drawing of a table. Measure it to find out how long and high the real table was (use the scale bar!).

As you make scale drawings of bigger and bigger things, the short length on the scale bar has to stand for longer and longer lengths in the real world. Otherwise the drawings would not fit on to pieces of paper that could be held easily. Look at the plan of the classroom. What scale is it drawn to? How long are the walls of the real classroom?

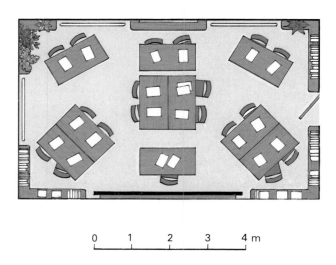

Cartographers (people who draw maps) make scale drawings of very big things – places and countries. So a small length on a map (for example 1 cm) has to stand for a very large one in real life (for example 1 km (100 000 cm) or 50 km (5 000 000 cm)). These examples could be written 1:100 000 or 1:5M (M stands for 'million'). When a scale is written like this, it is called a Representative Fraction (RF for short). Most maps have a scale bar as well as an RF. So if two places on a map are 6 cm apart and at the top of the page you see this:

1:5M | 0 ——— 50 ——— 100 ——— 150 ——— 200 km
         | 0 ——— 50 ——— 100 mls

you can work out that the real places are 300 km apart.

All the maps in this atlas have an RF and scale bar at the top of the page. The scale of the maps varies, depending on the size of the area each has to show.

MAP PROJECTIONS

People who make flat maps have one big problem: the world is spherical (like an orange). If you peel the skin off an orange

you will discover that you cannot make the pieces of skin lie flat unless you push them out of shape. In the same way, if map makers want to draw a flat map, they have to change the shapes or sizes (or both) of the countries on the surface of the earth. The only kind of map without these distortions (as the changes in shape and size are called) is a globe – a spherical map (right).

Over the centuries, many different ways of making flat maps of the earth have been discovered. They are called **Map Projections**. A projector makes an image on a screen by shining a light through a piece of film. Map makers pretended to shine a light through from the inside of the world and drew the outlines of countries as they would look on a flat surface. This type of map is called an **Azimuthal Projection**.

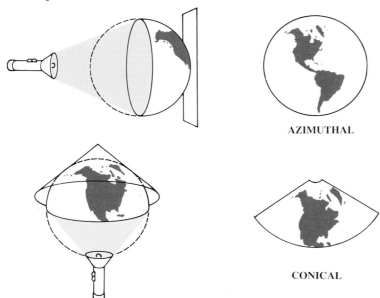

AZIMUTHAL

CONICAL

By 'shining a light' through different parts of the world (the top, the sides and so on) different maps could be drawn. The next step was to change the shape of the 'screen' onto which the outlines of countries were projected. Some map makers used a cone shape. Their maps are called **Conical Projections**. Others used a cylinder shape, as if a piece of paper had been wrapped round the world. A map made like this is called a **Cylindrical Projection**. Other ways of drawing maps were developed, which did not use this idea of 'shining a light', but they are all called 'projections' from the first way of drawing them.

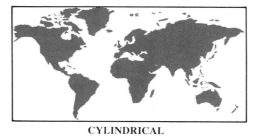

CYLINDRICAL

All projections distort land and sea areas and their positions in different ways. Map makers choose the projection they want to use depending on what the map is for. They consider things like relative sizes of areas, shapes of areas, directions and distances. Look at the box on the right, showing Australia drawn using three different projections (there are many more than that); see how different the shape of the country is.

THREE PROJECTIONS OF AUSTRALIA

INTERRUPTED SINUSOIDAL
Distances are accurate along all parallels of latitude and on each centre meridian.

PETERS PROJECTION
Modified Mercator projection (cylindrical) which tries to show the sizes of different countries in proportion to each other. Often used for maps showing the inequality of wealth distribution in proportion to country size and population.

MERCATOR
Distances are accurate but land areas are distorted; traditionally used for navigation; the most popular projection in the past for world maps.

6 WORLD MAP OF THE ENVIRONMENT

The world can be divided into 8 broad 'climatic zones' (these are areas with a particular sort of weather). The natural types of plants and animals found in each zone are different and depend on the weather the zone has. This map shows which parts of the world are in each zone. The colour of the strip at the top of each zone description (for example, Desert, Rainforest) is the same as the colour used for the zone on the big map. The little map beside each zone description pinpoints where that type of habitat is found in the world. (For example, the Desert strip is orange/yellow. The little sketch map shows you where on the big map to look for this colour. You will find this colour in the north of Africa, the west of North America and in parts of Asia and Australia. All these places have deserts. The description tells you what the natural countryside looks like and what plants and animals live there.)

SCRUB OR MEDITERRANEAN

Areas of long, hot, dry summers and short, warm winters. The land used to be covered with trees, but man cleared it for crops and grazed his animals on it. Now there is evergreen scrub – vines and olive trees.

TUNDRA OR MOUNTAIN

Polar areas which are usually frozen over. During the short summers the top layer of soil thaws, creating vast marshes. Compact, wind-resistant plants and lichens and mosses are found here. Animals include lemmings and reindeer.

NORTHERN FOREST (TAIGA)

Forests of conifers growing over a large area. Winters are very cold and long. Summers are short. Trees include spruce and fir. Animals found here include beavers, squirrels and red deer.

WOODLAND AND GRASS

Temperate areas (where the weather is seldom very cold or very hot). Deciduous trees (which lose their leaves in winter) grow in the woodlands. They include oak, beech and maple. Man uses these areas most of all, for farming, building towns and villages, and industry.

GRASSLAND

Hot summers, cold winters and moderate rainfall. Huge area of grassland and 'black' (very fertile) soils. Grain crops grow well, and so does rich pasture for beef cattle. Names for this kind of grassland include steppe, veld, pampas and prairie.

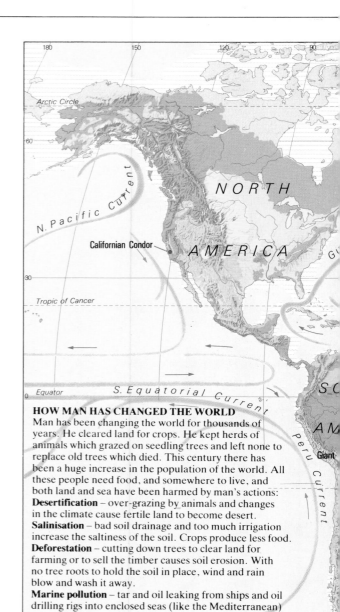

Arctic Circle

N. Pacific Current

Californian Condor

NORTH AMERICA

Tropic of Cancer

Equator

S. Equatorial Current

Peru Current

Giant

HOW MAN HAS CHANGED THE WORLD

Man has been changing the world for thousands of years. He cleared land for crops. He kept herds of animals which grazed on seedling trees and left none to replace old trees which died. This century there has been a huge increase in the population of the world. All these people need food, and somewhere to live, and both land and sea have been harmed by man's actions:

Desertification – over-grazing by animals and changes in the climate cause fertile land to become desert.

Salinisation – bad soil drainage and too much irrigation increase the saltiness of the soil. Crops produce less food.

Deforestation – cutting down trees to clear land for farming or to sell the timber causes soil erosion. With no tree roots to hold the soil in place, wind and rain blow and wash it away.

Marine pollution – tar and oil leaking from ships and oil drilling rigs into enclosed seas (like the Mediterranean) harm their plants and animals.

SAVANNA

Tall grasses with thick stems, and flat-topped thorny trees grow here. Animals grazing here include giraffes and zebras. There is a short rainy season. Often it does not rain for a long time (a drought). Fires burn the dried out plants but they have adapted to survive this and grow again.

DESERT

These areas have bare mountains, rocky wastes and sand dunes. Plants (wiry grass, thorn bushes and cacti) and animals (lizards and camels) must be well adapted to survive very high temperatures and little water. It may rain only once in several years.

North Pole

Arctic Circle

N. Atlantic Drift

European Bison

Abruzzo Brown Bear

EUROPE

Monk Seal

POLLUTION

AFRICA

DESERTIFICATION

DEFORESTATION

Guinea Current

Woolly Spider Monkey

Benguela Current

Brazil Current

Giant Anteater

Tropic of Capricorn

Arabian Oryx
Hunted by man

Monsoon Drift

(July)

Przewalski's Horse

Desertification

ASIA

Giant Panda

Bengal Tiger

Asiatic Lion
Last remnant

Orang-utan
Only great ape
outside C.Africa

Salinisation

(Jan)

Indian Counter Current

Equatorial Current (Jan)

Mountain Gorilla

Indris
Largest surviving lemur

DEFORESTATION

Kuro-Shio

N.Equatorial Current

Numbat
Marsupial

AUSTRALIA

Parma Wallaby
Last remnant

West Wind Drift

Takahe
Flightless bird

- ● Endangered wildlife
- Continental shelf
- Ice shelf

Ocean Circulation
→ Surface currents-warm
→ Surface currents-cold

South Pole

Antarctic Circle

RAINFOREST

Hot and wet, with no real winter or summer. Trees with thick foliage, climbing plants, monkeys and tigers are found here. There are five 'layers' of plants in a rainforest: the high trees, the tree canopy, the open canopy, shrubs and ground plants.

8 KEY MAP

This map shows you which part of the world is shown in each of the regional maps in this atlas. The area of each regional map is outlined in black (physical maps) or red (political maps). In the top right hand corner of each map box is a number (or two numbers) e.g. 16, 38-39. This is the number of the page or pages where you will find a map of the area within the black, or red-outlined box. The list below gives the name of each map.

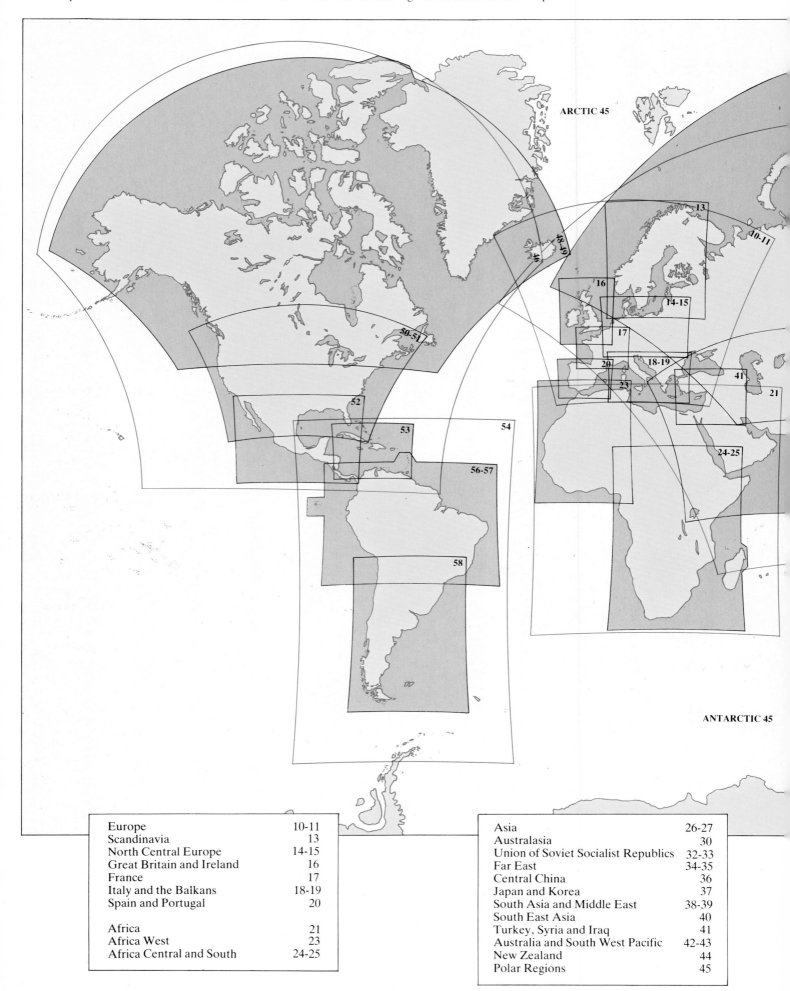

ARCTIC 45

ANTARCTIC 45

This panel explains the different lettering styles, the main symbols and the height and depth colours used on the reference maps in this atlas.

LETTERING STYLES

CANADA	Independent Nation
FLORIDA	State, Province or Autonomous Region
Gibraltar (U.K.)	Sovereignty of Dependent Territory
Lothian	Administrative Area
LANGUEDOC	Historic Region
Loire **Vosges**	Physical Feature or Physical Region

TOWNS AND CITIES

Square symbols mark capital cities

			Population
■	●	**New York**	over 5 000 000
■	●	**Montréal**	over 1 000 000
□	○	Ottawa	over 500 000
■	●	Québec	over 100 000
□	○	St John's	over 50 000

  Built-up-area

BOUNDARIES

━━━━	International
━ ━ ━	International under Dispute
┅┅┅	Cease Fire Line
————	Autonomous or State
————	Administrative
─ ─ ─	Maritime (National)
─ ─ ─	International Date Line

LANDSCAPE FEATURES

  Glacier, Ice Cap

Marsh, Swamp

Sand Desert, Dunes

LAKE FEATURES

	Freshwater
	Saltwater
	Seasonal
	Salt Pan

OTHER FEATURES

﹋	River
﹉﹍→	Seasonal River
⊐⊏	Pass, Gorge
	Dam, Barrage
﹋	Waterfall, Rapid
———┤├———	Aqueduct
﹏﹏	Reef
▲4231	Summit, Peak

Height

	6000m
	5000m
	4000m
	3000m
	2000m
	1000m
	500m
	200m

0 — Sea Level — 0

Depth

	200m
	2000m
	4000m
	6000m
	8000m

32-33
26-27
37
34-35
36
38-39
40
30
42-43
44

1:15M

5 Cork stack and cork oak tree, Portugal

8 Venice, Italy

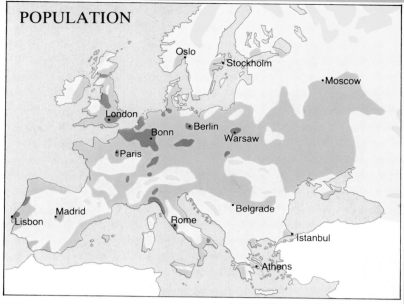

POPULATION

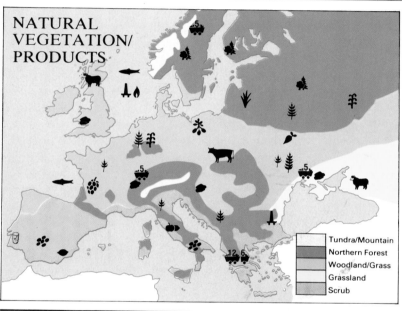

NATURAL VEGETATION/ PRODUCTS

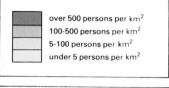

over 500 persons per km²	
100-500 persons per km²	
5-100 persons per km²	
under 5 persons per km²	

Cattle		Oil	
Sheep		Coal	
Fish		Gas	
Fruit		Oats	
Citrus fruit		Wheat	
Grapes		Maize	
Yams		Rye	
Sugar beet		Barley	
Potatoes		Minerals	
Timber		Iron	5
Cork		Lead	6
		Zinc	12

Tundra/Mountain
Northern Forest
Woodland/Grass
Grassland
Scrub

DID YOU KNOW THAT …?

1 In Iceland, ice and fire exist side by side! Many active volcanoes and geysers (hot springs which shoot a column of water into the air at intervals) can be seen, while glaciers (continually moving 'rivers' of ice) and ice sheets cover much of the land. One volcano – Vatnajokull – is particularly dangerous for an unusual reason: it is underneath a glacier and when it erupts, the ice melts very quickly, causing terrible floods.

2 The Humber Bridge, England, has the longest main span of any bridge in the world. It stretches for 1410 m (4626 feet).

3 More than a third of the land area of the Netherlands has been reclaimed from the sea! These lands (the *polders*) are below sea level and the sea is kept out by dykes. Drainage ditches divide the fertile fields. The water from them is pumped into canals and rivers, then out to sea.

4 The longest river in Europe is the Volga, which runs for 3690 km (2293 miles) from the forests north west of Moscow all the way to the Caspian Sea.

5 Portugal is an important source of cork, which is actually the bark of a tree! The cork oak produces cork bark up to 15 cm (6 inches) thick and this is stripped off the trees every 10 to 15 years. Cork oaks grow throughout the western and central Mediterranean region.

6 The Pierre Saint Martin Cavern in the Pyrenees mountains, France, is the deepest cave system yet discovered in the world. It goes 1330 m (4364 feet) into the heart of the mountains.

7 The principality of Monaco is one of the most crowded countries in the world: 28 000 people live on 1.9 sq km (467 acres) of land! By contrast, most of Scandinavia has fewer than 40 people per square kilometre!

8 Venice, Italy, is built on no less than 118 islands! Instead of roads, there are canals, and boats are used for transport. Venice is sinking at a rate of 12 inches each century. Some of the reasons for this include water being extracted from wells, and the compression of the mud on the floor of the lagoon.

9 Mount Etna, Sicily, is the highest volcano in Europe (about 3323 m, 10 902 ft) and is still very active. Despite this, many people live on its lower slopes! This is because the soil there is very fertile and grows good produce.

2 The Humber Bridge, England

AUSTRIA

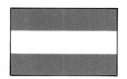

Area: 83 848 sq km
(32 374 sq miles)
Population: 7 600 000
Capital: Vienna
Language: German
Currency: Schilling

BELGIUM

Area: 30 512 sq km
(11 781 sq miles)
Population: 9 900 000
Capital: Brussels
Languages: Flemish, French
Currency: Belgian Franc

DENMARK

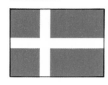

Area: 43 030 sq km
(16 614 sq miles)
Population: 5 100 000
Capital: Copenhagen
Language: Danish
Currency: Krone

EAST GERMANY

Area: 107 860 sq km
(41 645 miles)
Population: 16 700 000
Capital: Berlin (East)
Language: German
Currency: DDR Mark

FRANCE

Area: 551 000 sq km
(212 741 sq miles)
Population: 54 800 000
Capital: Paris
Language: French
Currency: Franc

GREECE

Area: 131 955 sq km
(50 948 sq miles)
Population: 10 000 000
Capital: Athens
Language: Greek
Currency: Drachma

IRELAND

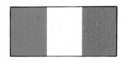

Area: 70 282 sq km
(27 136 sq miles)
Population: 3 600 000
Capital: Dublin
Languages: Irish (Gaelic),
English
Currency: Irish Pound
(Punt)

ITALY

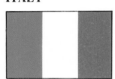

Area: 301 245 sq km
(116 311 sq miles)
Population: 57 000 000
Capital: Rome
Language: Italian
Currency: Lira

NETHERLANDS

Area: 33 940 sq km
(13 104 sq miles)
Population: 14 400 000
Capital: The Hague
Language: Dutch
Currency: Guilder

POLAND

Area: 312 683 sq km
(120 727 sq miles)
Population: 36 900 000
Capital: Warsaw
Language: Polish
Currency: Zloty

PORTUGAL

Area: 91 671 sq km
(35 394 sq miles)
Population: 10 100 000
Capital: Lisbon
Language: Portuguese
Currency: Escudo

SPAIN

Area: 504 745 sq km
(194 882 sq miles)
Population: 38 400 000
Capital: Madrid
Language: Spanish
Currency: Peseta

UNITED KINGDOM

Area: 244 104 sq km
(94 249 sq miles)
Population: 56 000 000
Capital: London
Language: English
Currency: Pound Sterling

WEST GERMANY

Area: 248 528 sq km
(95 957 sq miles)
Population: 61 400 000
Capital: Bonn
Language: German
Currency: Deutschmark

YUGOSLAVIA

Area: 255 803 sq km
(98 766 sq miles)
Population: 23 000 000
Capital: Belgrade
Languages: Serbo-Croatian,
Macedonian, Slovenian
Currency: Dinar

10 Monasteries on rock pillars,
Greece

10 Near Kalabaka, Greece, are
group of monasteries built fo
monks with no fear of height
They are perched on top of pilla
of rock, called meteora, 300
(1 000 ft) high! The only way u
was by ladders or baskets slung c
the end of ropes. Now stairwa
have been constructed so that tou
ists can visit the buildings.

11 The island of Santorini (Thira
in Greece is the site of t
world's largest natural disaste
About 1500 BC this volcanic islan
erupted leaving a *caldera* (hollo
basin shape where the top of t
volcano had been) about 13 km
miles) across. Many people believ
that the destruction of this island
the origin of the story of Atlanti
The people of Atlantis are mer
tioned by the Greek writer Plat
Crime and corruption sprea
throughout their island as th
became wealthier, until finally t
Athenians conquered them. Lat
the island disappeared into the s
in a single day and night.

7 Monte Carlo, Monaco

1:7.5M

100   200   300 km
50   100   150 mls

A   20   B   15   C

Arctic Circle

ICELAND

Akureyri

Vatnajökull

Reykjavik

e same scale

D Færøerne
(Den.)

Torshavn

E

the scale

7W   5

ARCTIC OCEAN

Arctic Circle

N O R W E G I A N   S E A

Lofoten   Vesterålen

Narvik

Vestfjorden

Bodø

Trondheimsfj.

Trondheim

Östersund

Sundsvall

Glittertind.
2470

Songnefjorden

Bergen

Hardangerfj.

Oslo

Stavanger

Kristiansand

S k a g e r r a k

Göteborg   Jönköping

Vänern

Ålborg

Kattegat

North

Sea

Århus   Helsingborg

DENMARK

Esbjerg

Copenhagen
(København)

Odense   Malmö

Bornholm
(Den.)

Gulf of
Gdansk

Kiel

Wilhelmshaven   Rostock

Hamburg

Bremen

WEST

Elbe

Hannover   Berlin

GERMANY   EAST

Szczecin

POLAND

Poznań

Warsaw
(Warszawa)

H   20   J   25   K   30   L   35   M

BARENTS
SEA

Murmansk

Kol'skiy
Poluostrov

Ivalo

Kemijärvi

Gällivare

Luleå

Oulu

Karel'skaya
A.S.S.R.

Vaasa

FINLAND

Tampere

Ladozhskoye
Ozero

Gulf of Bothnia

Turku

Helsinki
(Helsingfors)

Leningrad

Uppsala

Tallinn

Stockholm

Gulf of Finland

Norrköping

Gulf of
Riga

ESTONSKAYA
S.S.R.

ROSSIYSKAYA
S.F.S.R.

Gotland

Riga   LATVIYSKAYA
S. S. R.

B A L T I C   S E A

LITOVSKAYA
S. S. R.

Kaliningrad

Gdansk

S W E D E N

N O R W A Y

Vänern

Arctic Circle

ARCTIC OCEAN

65

70

70

65

60

55

4

5

6

7

8

1:5M

0		50		100		150		200 km
0		50			100 mls			

Ⓐ   5   Ⓑ   10   Ⓒ

①

55

N O R T H

S E A

②

Göteborg ●   Jönköping ●

S W E D E N

Ålborg ●

K a t t e g a t

Århus ●

D E N M A R K

Jutland
(Jylland)

Helsingborg ●

Esbjerg ○

Odense ●

Sjælland

Copenhagen ■
(København)

Malmö ●

Fyn

Lolland

B A L

B

Schleswig-Holstein

Elbe

Hamburg ●

Bremen ●

N I E D E R S A C H S E N

Elbe

E A S T

G E R M A N Y

Oder
(Odra)

Po

The Hague □
('s-Gravenhage)

Amsterdam ●

Ijsselmeer

N E T H E R L A N D S

Hannover ●

Berlin ■

Rotterdam ●

Maas

Rhein

NORDRHEIN-

Lippe

Leipzig ○

○ *Zeebrugge*

Antwerp ●

Schelde

Duisburg ○ ○ **Dortmund**
○ **Essen**

○ **Dunkerque**

B E L G I U M

Düsseldorf
WESTFALEN

Ruhr

Dresden ○

Elbe

Brussels ■
(Brüssel/
Bruxelles)

Cologne ●
(Köln)

Bonn ■

Lille ●

50

H E S S E N

W E S T

Wr
(B

Ardennes

Frankfurt ○

LUXEM
BOURG

Mosel

RHEINLAND
PFALZ

● Luxembourg

SAAR-
LAND

● Reims

Prague ■
(Praha)

C Z E

G E R M A N Y

○ **Nürnberg**

Č E S K É Z E M É

CHAMPAGNE

F R A N C E

L O R R A I N E

Seine

B A D E N **B A Y E R N**

Stuttgart ○

Dijon ●

③

Saône

Vosges

ALSACE

Schwarzwald

WÜRTTEMBURG

Danube

Munich ●
(München)

Danube

Vienn
(Wien
■

B O U R G O G N E

FRANCHE-COMTÉ

Jura

Zürich ○

LIECHTEN
STEIN

Vaduz □

Salzburg ●

Innsbruck ●

A U S T R I A

■ Bern

Rhein

Brenner
1370

Grossglockner
3798

S

SWITZERLAND

Jungfrau
4158

▲ *2112*
St Gotthard

Geneva ●
(Genève)

Rhône

Simplon
2009

▲ *Matterhorn*
4477

L

P

SAVOIE

4807
▲ *Mt*
Blanc

I T A L Y

Alpi Dolomitiche

Ljubljana ●

Lyon ●

DAUPHINÉ

45

● Grenoble

Milan ●
(Milano)

Venice ○
(Venezia)

G. di
Venezia

Zagreb ○

④

Rhône

Turin ●
(Torino)

Y U

Ⓐ   5   Ⓑ   10   15

Gulf of Riga

Riga

LATVIYSKAYA S.S.R.

Velikiye-Luki

R.S.F.S.R.

Daugavpils

LITOVSKAYA
S. S. R.

Smolensk

Gulf of
Gdańsk

R.S.F.S.R.

Gdynia

Vilnius

Minsk

BELORUSSKAYA
S.S.R.

Dneprovskaya

Bobruysk

Dnepr

Białystok

Gomel

L A N D

Nizmennost'

Dnepr

Vistula (Wisła)

Warsaw
(Warszawa)

Brest

Łódź

U. S. S. R.

Wisła

Lublin

Kiyev

Dnepr

L'vov

Chorzow

Kraków

U K R A I N S K A Y A

Podol'skaya
S. S. R.

Pridneprovskaya Vozv.

Vozv

Dnestr

L O V A K I A

LOVENSKO

Košice

MOLDAVSKAYA

Nyíregyháza

Carpatii Orientali

Budapest

Baia Mare

Dnestr

N G A R Y

Odessa

Cluj-Napoca

Bacău

S. S. R.

Szeged

Arad

Black Sea

A V I A

Novi Sad

R O M A N I A

Transylvanian Alps
(Mtii Carpatii Meridionali)

1:5M

0   50   100   150   200 km
0   50   100 mls

Ⓐ   10   Ⓑ   5   Ⓒ   Ⓓ   Ⓔ

① 60   NORWAY

Shetland

② *Orkney*

C. Wrath

Outer Hebrides

The Minch

○ Inverness
L. Ness

● Aberdeen

SCOTLAND

Ben Nevis 1344

● Dundee

Grampian Mts

L. Lomond

Glasgow ●   ○ Edinburgh

Clyde

NORTH

SEA

55

● Newcastle-upon-Tyne

Londonderry ○   **N. IRELAND**   Stranraer ○
○ Larne

Cheviots

L. Neagh   **Belfast** ●

Scafell Pike 977 ▲

Pennines

● Middlesbrough

Isle of Man

IRISH SEA

● **Leeds**

Galway ○

Shannon

Dublin □
(Baile Átha Cliath) Holyhead ○

Liverpool ●   ● **Manchester**
○ **Sheffield**

REP. OF
IRELAND

Wicklow Mts

▲1085
Snowdon

Cambrian Mts

③   **WALES**   **Birmingham** ●

E N G L A N D

Norwich ●

The Wash

Cork ●

St George's Chan.

Swansea ●
Cardiff ○   ○ **Bristol**

Thames

London
□

Harwich ●

NETHERLA

The Hague
('s-Gravenhage)
Rotterd

Zeebrugge ○

○ Dover

Antw

BELGIUM

● Southampton

Calais ○   ○ Dunkerque   **Brusse**
(Brüsse
Bruxell

Boulogne ●   **Lille** ●

Plymouth ●

A R T O I S

50   *Land's End*

English   Channel

P I C A R D I E

○ Cherbourg   Le Havre ●

④ 10   *Channel Is*
(U.K.)

N O R M A N D I E

□ **Paris**

Roscoff ○

F R A N C E

Ⓑ   5   Ⓒ   Ⓓ

1:5M

EAST GERMANY

WEST GERMANY

Düsseldorf
Cologne (Köln)
Bonn
Frankfurt
Nürnberg
Stuttgart
Munich (München)

AUSTRIA
Innsbruck
Vaduz
LIECHTEN STEIN

Milan (Milano)
Bologna
Florence (Firenze)
Livorno
Elba
Bastia

CORSICA (CORSE)

Genoa (Genova)
Ligurian Sea
Turin (Torino)

Zürich
Schwarzwald
SWITZERLAND
Bern
JURA
ALPS
Mt. Blanc 4807

Monte Carlo
MONACO
Nice
Côte d'Azur

Antwerp
Brussels (Brüssel/Bruxelles)
BELGIUM
LUXEMBOURG
Luxembourg
Metz
Strasbourg
ALSACE
VOSGES
LORRAINE
Ardennes

Geneva (Genève)
SAVOIE
Grenoble
DAUPHINÉ
PROVENCE

Dunkerque
Lille
Calais
Dover
Boulogne
ARTOIS
PICARDIE
Reims
CHAMPAGNE
Paris
Dijon
Saône
BOURGOGNE
NIVERNAIS
BERRY
Saône
Seine

Lyon
St-Étienne
Rhône
AUVERGNE
Massif Central
LANGUEDOC
Marseille
Golfe du Lion

Plymouth
Portsmouth
ENGLAND
English Channel
Cherbourg
Le Havre
Rouen
Seine
NORMANDIE
MAINE
ANJOU
ORLÉANAIS
Tours
POITOU
LIMOUSIN
Limoges
FRANCE
Channel Is (U.K.)

Roscoff
Brest
BRETAGNE
Nantes

BAY OF BISCAY

GUYENNE
Bordeaux
GASCOGNE
Toulouse
Pyrénées
ROUSSILLON
ANDORRA

Bilbao
VASCONGADAS
NAVARRA
SPAIN
ASTURIAS

1:5M

| 0 | 50 | 100 | 150 | 200 km |

| 0 | 50 | 100 mls |

Ⓐ 5 Ⓑ 10 Ⓒ 15 B

Munich
(München)

WEST GERMANY

Salzburg

Vienna
(Wien)

Basel

Zürich○

Bern

LIECHTEN
STEIN

Innsbruck

Vaduz○

Brenner
1370

A U S T R I A

Graz

①

J
u
r
a

S W I T Z E R L A N D

2112 St Gotthard

Simplon
2009

Matterhorn
4477

Geneva
(Genève)

Lyon●

Mt
Blanc

St Bernard

P   S

Alpi Dolomitiche

Ljubljana●

○**Zagreb**

F R A N C E

Col du
Mt Cenis
2803

Milan
(Milano)●

Verona●

Venice (Venezia)
G. di
Venezia

C R O A T I A

Turin
(Torino)●

I

V
e
l
e
b
i
t

Y
U

D
A
L
M

Genoa
(Genova)○

A
P
T
P
e
n

Florence
(Firenze)●

SAN
MARINO

A
D
R
I
A
T
I
C

MONACO

L i g u r i a n
S e a

Livorno●

n
i

Ancona●

Split
(Spalat

Marseille○

②

a

Bastia●

Elba

A
p
e

Civitavecchia○

Pescara●

n

Ajaccio●

CORSICA
(CORSE)

Rome
(Roma)■

n
i
n
e
s

L
e

○ Sassari ●

Olbia○

Naples (Napoli)●

Vesuvio
1277

40

S A R D I N I A
(SARDEGNA)

T Y R R H E N I A N   S E A

Cosenza●

Cagliari●

Stromboli

S I C I L Y
(S I C I L I A)

Messina●

M
E
D
I
T
E
R
R
A
N

Palermo○

Reggio di Calabria●

③

Etna
3323▲

Bone
('Annaba)●

Syracuse
(Siracusa)●

Constantine○

Tunis□

A L G E R I A

T U N I S I A

E
A
N

MALTA

Ⓑ 10 Ⓒ 15 S

Baia Mare

Cluj-Napoca

Bacău

Odessa

U.S.S.R.

Budapest

nya

cs

Szeged

ROMANIA

Carp Orientali

Transylvanian Alps
(Mtii Carpatii Meridionali)

45

Novi Sad

Danube

Belgrade
(Beograd)

Bucharest
(Bucuresti)

Constanţa

Craiova

SLAVIA

Ruse

Sarajevo

SERBIA

Pleven

Varna

BLACK
SEA

②

Niš

Stara Planina

BULGARIA

MONTENEGRO

Sofiya

vnik

Plovdiv

Scutari
(Shkoder)

Skopje

Bosporus
(Karadeniz Boğazi)

ALBANIA

Istanbul

Sea of Marmara

Tiranë

A

Salonica
(Thessaloniki)

Balıkesir

40

Olympus
(Olimbos)
2917▲

Kalabáka

Píndhos

TURKEY

Kerkira
Corfu
(Kérkira)

GREECE

AEGEAN
SEA

Izmir

IONIAN ISLANDS
(IONIOI NISOI)

Denizli

③

Pátrai

Athens
(Athínai)

Piraiévs

IONIAN SEA

Cyclades
(Kikládhes)

DODECANESE
(SPORÁDHES)

Mirtoan
Sea

Thíra

Ródhos

Kríti

Iráklion

35

④

1:5M

50   100   150   200 km

50   100 mls

① 40 ②
35

D

Marseille○

Perpignan○

Costa Brava

BALEARIC ISLANDS
(ISLAS BALEARES)

Menorca

Algiers
(Alger)

C

Barcelona

Tarragona

Mallorca

Palma
de Mallorca

F R A N C E

ANDORRA

Andorra○
La V.

Pyrénées

Pirineos

C A T A L U Ñ A

Lérida

A
R
A
G
Ó
N

Zaragoza

Ibiza

Castellon de la P.

Valencia

Alicante

Costa Blanca

MEDITERRANEAN SEA

Oran

ALGERIA

Melilla (Sp.)

BAY OF BISCAY

NAVARRA

Bilbao○

VASCONGADAS

Santander

Cantábrica

Cordillera

Burgos

CASTILLA LA VIEJA

Madrid■

NUEVA

Albacete

MURCIA

Murcia

La Mancha

M
o
r
e
n
a

Granada

Sa Nevada

Córdoba

Malaga

Costa del Sol

Costa de la Luz

Gibraltar (U.K.)

○Gibraltar

Str. of Gibraltar

S

P

A

La Coruña

GALICIA

Oviedo●

ASTURIAS

León

D
U
E
R
O

Valladolid

CASTILLA

LA

E X T R E M A D U R A

Badajoz

S i e r r a

A
N
D
A
L
U
C
I
A

Seville
(Sevilla)

Cádiz

Tangier
(Tanger)

P
O
R
T
U
G
A
L

Oporto
(Porto)

Tagus (Tejo)

Faro○

Lisbon
(Lisboa)

MOROCCO

① 40 ②

10

400   800   1200   1600 km
400   800 mis

1 Bedouin tent in the Sahara

FINLAND
SWEDEN
Helsinki
Stockholm
Göteborg   Baltic Sea
Riga   Leningrad   Gor'kiy
Volga
Minsk   Moscow
Berlin   Warsaw
Gdańsk
POLAND   Kiev   Kharkov
Prague   Kraków   Dnepr
CZECHOSLOVAKIA   Rostov
Vienna   Odessa
AUSTRIA   HUNGARY   Budapest
Belgrade   ROMANIA
YUGOSLAVIA   Sofia   Bucharest   Black Sea
Adriatic Sea   BULGARIA   Danube
Tirana   Istanbul
ALB.   Ankara
Naples   GREECE   Athens   TURKEY
Kriti
CYPRUS   Nicosia
SYRIA   Tabriz   Tehrān
Beirūt   Damascus   Baghdād   IRAN
LEB.   IRAQ
Jerusalem   Amman   Euphrates   Shīrāz   AFGHANISTAN
Port Said   ISR.   JORDAN   Basra   The Gulf   PAK.
Suez   KUWAIT   Kuwait   BAHRAIN   Abū   Muscat
Alexandria   Riyadh   QATAR   Dhabi
Cairo   SAUDI   Doha   UNITED ARAB   OMAN
Asyūt   Nile   EMIRATES
Aswān   ARABIA
L. Nasser   Mecca   Kuria Muria Is
Wadi Halfa   Red Sea   OMAN
Port Sudan
Omdurman   Atbara   San'á   YEMEN   SOUTH YEMEN   Socotra (S.Y.)
Khartoum   Kassala   Asmara   Aden   Gulf of Aden
El Obeid   Blue Nile   Djibouti   Hargeysa
SUDAN   White Nile   Addis Ababa   Dire Dawa
Wau   Jimma   ETHIOPIA   SOMALIA
CENTRAL   Juba   L. Rudolf   Mogadishu
AFRICAN REPUBLIC   Bambari   Gulu   UGANDA   L. Albert   Kampala   KENYA   Kismaayo
Ngaoundéré   Bangui   Kisangani   L. Edward   Entebbe   Nairobi
CAMEROON   Goma   RWANDA   Kigali   Lake Victoria   Mombasa
Douala   Mbandaka   Kindu   BURUNDI   Mwanza
Yaoundé   Zaire (Congo)   Bujumbura   Arusha
Bioko   Malabo   Kigoma   Dodoma
EQUAT. GUINEA   GABON   CONGO   Congo   Kalémié   TANZANIA   Dar es Salaam
SÃO TOMÉ & PRINCIPE   Libreville   Bandundu   Ilebo   Lake   Zanzibar
Príncipe   Lambaréné   ZAIRE   Lualaba   Tanganyika
São Tomé   Pagalu (Eq.G)   Brazzaville   Kananga   Kamina   Mbeya
Cabinda (Ang.)   Kinshasa   Mbuji-Mayi   Mbala
Matadi   Kasai   Ruvuma   COMOROS
Luanda   Malanje   Lubumbashi   MALAWI   Antserarana   Mayotte (Fr.)
Lobito   Bié   Ndola   Lake Nyasa   Moçambique   Mahajanga
ANGOLA   Lichinga   Nampula
Moçâmedes   ZAMBIA   Lilongwe   Zomba
Lusaka   MOZAMBIQUE   Toamasina
Cuando   L. Kariba   Zambezi   Antananarivo
Kunene   Zambezi   Harare   Mutare   MADAGASCAR
Okavango   ZIMBABWE   Sofala   MAURITIUS
Hwange   Gwero   Réunion (Fr.)
Tsumeb   Bulawayo   Inhambane   Toliara
Walvis Bay (S.A.)   BOTSWANA   Serowe   Limpopo   Mozambique Channel
Windhoek   Maputo
NAMIBIA (S.W. AFRICA)   Gaborone
Pretoria   Mbabane
Keetmanshoop   Johannesburg   SWAZILAND   Tropic of Capricorn
SOUTH   Kimberley   Maseru   LESOTHO
Orange   Bloemfontein   Durban
AFRICA
Cape Town   Port Elizabeth   East London

EUROPE   ASIA
AFRICA
Atlantic Ocean   Indian Ocean
SOUTH AMERICA

2 The River Nile, Aswan, Egypt

Madeira (Port.)
Tangier   Algiers   Mediterranean Sea
Rabat   Oran   Annaba   Sicilia
Fès   Constantine   Tunis   Sfax
Casablanca   TUNISIA   Tripoli
Marrakech   Béchar   Ghudamis   Benghāzi
MOROCCO   In Salah
Islas Canarias (Sp.)   La'youn   ALGERIA   Sabha   LIBYA
Tindouf   Tropic of Cancer   Ghāt
F'dérik   Tamanrasset   EGYPT
Nouadhibou   SAHARA   NIGER
MAURITANIA   Tombouctou   Agadez
Nouakchott   Niamey   CHAD
St Louis   Sénégal   MALI   N'Djamena
SENEGAL   Niger   Bamako   BURKINA (UPPER VOLTA)   Kano   Maiduguri
Banjul   GUINEA   Ouagadougou   Kaduna
GUINEA BISSAU   Kankan   Bobo Dioulasso   NIGERIA   CAMEROON
Conakry   Tamale   Ilorin   Niger
SIERRA LEONE   Kumasi   BENIN   Ibadan
Freetown   IVORY COAST   GHANA   TOGO   Onitsha
Monrovia   Bouaké   Volta   Porto Novo   Lagos
LIBERIA   Abidjan   Accra   Lomé   Port Harcourt
Buchanan   Gulf of Guinea

SOUTH ATLANTIC OCEAN

INDIAN OCEAN
Seychelles Arch.
Amirante Is
SEYCHELLES
Aldabra Is
Farquhar Is
Tromelin (Fr.)

4 Mount Kilimanjaro, Tanzania

POPULATION

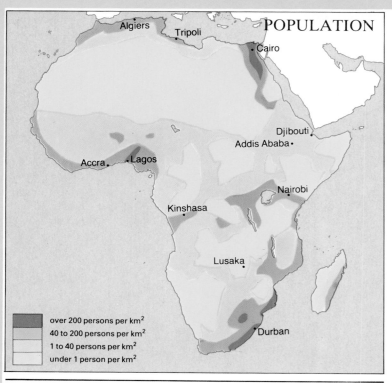

Algiers
Tripoli
Cairo
Djibouti
Addis Ababa
Accra
Lagos
Nairobi
Kinshasa
Lusaka
Durban

over 200 persons per km²
40 to 200 persons per km²
1 to 40 persons per km²
under 1 person per km²

NATURAL VEGETATION PRODUCTS

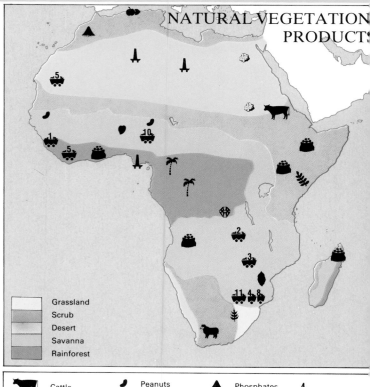

Grassland
Scrub
Desert
Savanna
Rainforest

🐄 Cattle	Peanuts	▲ Phosphates	4. Gold		
🐑 Sheep	Palm oil	Maize	5. Iron		
Cocoa	Tea	Minerals	8. Platinum		
Coffee	Tobacco	1. Bauxite	10. Tin		
Cotton	Diamonds	2. Cobalt	11. Uranium		
Fruit	Oil	3. Copper			

DID YOU KNOW THAT ...?

1 The largest desert in the world is the Sahara, but only about 30% of it is sand! The rest is rocky waste. People live mainly near oases, where the land is watered by springs rising to the surface and crops can be grown. The desert is very hot and dry, but there are a few plants and animals (like camels) specially adapted to these conditions.

2 The Nile is the longest river in the world and flows for 6650 km (4132 miles) through North Africa to the Mediterranean Sea.

The Nile used to flood its banks each year, but now the High Dam at Aswan controls the floods. When the dam was built, the temples of Abu Simbel (3000 years old) were moved to a higher site to stop them being flooded.

3 Some parts of Africa have had no rain, or very little, for several years. Food crops have failed and many people have died from malnutrition and starvation. A further problem has been wars, which have driven many people from their homes and fields. Even if part of a country can grow food, it is difficult to move that food into areas where none can be grown. There are few lorries and, where people are at war, transporting food may be dangerous. Although western countries have sent food supplies, there is still not enough to feed the hundreds of thousands of people who are starving. Governments are trying to find ways growing more food and distributi it more quickly.

4 Kilimanjaro (now rename Uhuru, meaning 'freedom') the highest mountain in Afri (5895 m; 19 340 feet) and its pea are always covered in snow.

EGYPT

Area: 1 000 250 sq km (386 197 sq miles)
Population: 47 000 000
Capital: Cairo
Language: Arabic
Currency: Egyptian Pound

ETHIOPIA

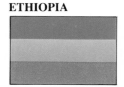

Area: 1 221 918 sq km (471 783 sq miles)
Population: 32 000 000
Capital: Addis Ababa
Language: Amharic
Currency: Birr

KENYA

Area: 582 644 sq km (224 959 sq miles)
Population: 19 400 000
Capital: Nairobi
Languages: English, Swahili
Currency: Kenya Shilling

LIBYA

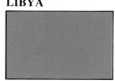

Area: 1 759 530 sq km (679 355 sq miles)
Population: 3 700 000
Capital: Tripoli
Language: Arabic
Currency: Libyan Dinar

NIGERIA

Area: 923 769 sq km (356 667 sq miles)
Population: 88 100 000
Capital: Lagos
Language: English
Currency: Naira

SOUTH AFRICA

Area: 1 221 038 sq km (471 443 sq miles)
Population: 31 700 000
Capital: Pretoria
Languages: Afrikaans, English
Currency: Rand

SUDAN

Area: 2 505 792 sq km (967 486 sq miles)
Population: 21 000 000
Capital: Khartoum
Language: Arabic
Currency: Sudanese Pound

ZAIRE

Area: 2 344 885 sq km (905 360 sq miles)
Population: 32 200 000
Capital: Kinshasa
Language: French
Currency: Zaire

1:15M

200   400   600 km
100   200   300 mls

30 w

Azores
(Acores)

Madeira
(Portugal)

20

Canary Islands
(Islas Canarias)
(Spain)

Lisbon
(Lisboa)
PORTUGAL

SPAIN

Seville
(Sevilla)

Str. of
Gibraltar   Gibraltar (U.K.)
Tangiers   Ceuta (Sp.)
(Tanger)   Tetouan

Melilla
(SP.)

Mostaganem   El
Asnam

Algiers
(Alger)

Skikda
(Philippeville)   Bône
('Annaba)

Tunis

Batna

Casablanca
(El-Dar-El-Beida)   Rabat
Meknès

Marrakech

Tlemcen

Laghouat

TUNISIA

M O R O C C O

Haut   Atlas

Béchar

Ouargla

Grand Erg Occidental

El Golea

Grand erg Oriental

30

La'youn

Tinfouchy

Western Sahara

Erg   Iguidi

A L G E R I A

Reggane

In Salah

Bir Moghrein

Tropic of Cancer

S   A   H   A   R   A

2

MAURITANIA

El   Djouf

Troudenni

El Khenachich

Tamanrasset

Tassili du Hoggar

Tessalit

20

kchott

MALI

N I G E R

SENEGAL

Niger

Mopti

Tahoua

Zinder

3

Bamako

BURKINA
(UPPER VOLTA)

Niamey

Sokoto

GUINEA

Volta Noire

Ouagadougou

Volta Blanche

Kano

Kankan

Bobo
Dioulasso

Bolgatanga

Kaduna

Conakry

Black Volta

White
Volta

NIGERIA

SIERRA
LEONE

Tamale

10

Freetown

IVORY
COAST

TOGO

GHANA

BENIN

Ibadan

Bouaké

L.
Volta

Benin
City

Enugu

LIBERIA

Kumasi

Lagos

Monrovia

Abidjan

Accra

Lomé   Porto
Novo

Port
Harcourt

CAMEROON

Takoradi

Bight of Benin

Mouths
of the R.Niger

Niger

Douala

4

Yaoundé

Bight of
Biafra

EQUATORIAL
GUINEA

Bata

GULF OF GUINEA

S.TOME &
PRINCIPE

Libreville

25w

APE VERDE

Equator

10

1:15M

200   400   600 km
100   200   300 mls

SAUDI ARABIA

YEMEN

San'ā

Al Hudaydah (Hodeida)

Ta'izz

Aden (Adan)

Gulf of Aden

Berbera

Hargeysa

DJIBOUTI

Djibouti

Mecca

Jiddah

RED SEA

Port Sudan

Asmara

Kassala

Atbara

Khartoum

Wad Medani

Omdurman

El Obeid

Nubian Desert

Wadi Halfa

Nile

Gondar

Dessye

ETHIOPIA

Addis Ababa

Yirga Alem

Jimma

Harar

Lake Rudolf

KENYA

Mt Kenya △ 5209

Kilimanjaro △ 5895

Nairobi

Masai Steppe

Mombasa

SOMALI

Mogadishu (Muqdisho)

Markao

Belet Uen

Kismaayo

INDIAN

Equator

Malakal

Juba

Wau

Kenamuke Swamp

Gulu

UGANDA

Kampala

Lake Victoria

RWANDA

Kigali

BURUNDI

Bujumbura

Bukavu

Lake

Kisangani (Stanleyville)

Isiro

SUDAN

En Nahud

LIBYA

Dépression du Mourdi

Geneina

Abéché

CHAD

Tibesti

NIGER

Plateau du Diado

Grand Erg de Bilma

Zinder

Kano

Maiduguri

N'Djamena (Ft Lamy)

Lake Chad

NIGERIA

CENTRAL AFRICAN REPUBLIC

Dar Rounga

Bangassou

Gemena

Bangui

Doba

Berbérati

Bouar

Ngaoundéré

CAMEROON

Yaoundé

Douala

Bata

EQUATORIAL GUINEA

Bight of Biafra

Libreville

Port Gentil

GABON

CONGO

Brazzaville

Kinshasa (Léopoldville)

ZAIRE

Mbandaka (Coquilhatville)

Congo

Luobomo

Tchibanga

Pte Noire

OCEAN

SEYCHELLES

COMOROS

OCEAN

Mahajanga
(Majunga)

MADAGASCAR
(MALAGASY REP.)

Mozambique Channel

Antananarivo
(Tananarive)

Fianarantsoa

Toamasina
(Tamatave)

Antananarivo
(Tananarive)

Mahajanga
(Majunga)

Fianarantsoa

Toliara

Tropic of Capricorn

MADAGASCAR
(MALAGASY REP.)

at the same scale 50

Mtwara

Pemba

Nampula

Sumbawanga

K-8

Kasama

Mbamba Bay

L. Nyasa

MALAWI

Lilongwe

Blantyre

Chipata

Teteo

Quelimane

Sofala (Beira)

MOZAMBIQUE

Inhambane

Xai Xai

Mabalane

60E

MAURITIUS

Durban

Likasi
(Jadotville)

Lubumbashi
(Elisabethville)

Mufulira

Ndola

Chililabombwe

Luanshya

Kamina

Kapiri

ZAMBIA

Lusaka

Mazabuka

Harare
(Salisbury)

Mutare

ZIMBABWE

Nyanda

Bulawayo

Maputo
(Lourenço Marques)

SWAZI-LAND

NATAL

TRANSVAAL

Pretoria

Johannesburg

Drakensberg

East London

Mongu

Kariba Dam

Zambezi

Maramba
(Livingstone)

Victoria Falls

Francistown

Maun

BOTSWANA

Kalahari Desert

Mahalapye

Gaborone

ORANGE FREE STATE

Welkom

Kimberley

Bloemfontein

LESOTHO

Orange

SOUTH AFRICA

CAPE PROVINCE

Capenda Camulemba

Malange

ANGOLA

Huambo
(Nova Lisboa)

Cuchi

Lubango

Lobito

Luanda

Tsumeb

Zambezi

NAMIBIA
(S. W. AFRICA)

Namib Desert

Windhoek

Walvis Bay
(SA)

Keetmanshoop

Orange

Desert

Cape Town
Table Mtn 1087▲
Cape of Good Hope

Tropic of Capricorn

ATLANTIC OCEAN

OCEAN

400
800
1200
1600 km
0
400
800 mils

ARCTIC OCEAN

6 The bullet train and Mount Fuji-san, Japan

ICELAND
IRELAND
Dublin
Edinburgh
London
UNITED KINGDOM
NETH.
BEL.
FRANCE
Paris
GERMANY
DENMARK
Copenhagen
NORWAY
Oslo
Faeroerne (Den.)
SWEDEN
Stockholm
Helsinki
FINLAND
Riga
Murmansk
Arkhangel'sk
Vorkuta
SWITZ.
AUSTRIA
Marseille
ITALY
Corse (Fr.)
Rome
Sardegna
Sicily
Tunis
CZECHOSLOVAKIA
HUNGARY
POLAND
Warsaw
YUGOSLAVIA
ROMANIA
Bucharest
ALB.
BULGARIA
GREECE
Athens
Kiev
Odessa
Khar'kov
Rostov
Black Sea
Leningrad
Moscow
Gorkiy
UNION OF SOVIET SOCIALIST REPUBL
Volga
Kuybyshev
Astrakhan'
Sverdlovsk
Chelyabinsk
Omsk
Ob'
Yenisey
Krasnoyarsk
Novosibirsk
Irkutsk
Yakutsk
Lena
Novosibirskiye Ostrova
Arctic Circle

1
2
3

SPAIN
PORT

TURKEY
Istanbul
Ankara
Adana
CYPRUS
Beirut
LEB.
Halab
SYRIA
Damascus
Jerusalem
ISRAEL
JOR.
Amman
Baghdad
IRAQ
Basra
KUWAIT
Caspian Sea
Baku
Tabriz
Tehrān
Mosul
Esfahān
Mashhad
Herat
Kabul
Kermān
Ashkhabad
Aral Sea
Tashkent
Alma Ata
Ürümqi
SINKIANG
MONGOLIA
Ulaanbaatar
INNER MONGO
Taiyuan
Lanzhou
Zhengh
Xi'an
CHINA
Chengdu
Chongqing
Chang Jiang

5
4

LIBYA
Alexandria
Cairo
EGYPT
Aswān
Nile
SUDAN
Khartoum
Asmara
ETHIOPIA
Addis Ababa
DJIBOUTI
Adan
G. of Aden
SOMALIA
Mogadishu
KENYA
Mombasa
Dar es Salaam
TANZANIA
MOZAMBIQUE
COMOROS
Aldabra Is (Sey.)
MADAGASCAR
Antananarivo
Equator

RED SEA
Mecca
SAUDI ARABIA
Riyadh
BAHRAIN
QATAR
Abū Dhabi
U.A.E.
The Gulf
Muscat
OMAN
YEMEN
San'ā
S. YEMEN
Socotra (S.Yemen)
AFGHANISTAN
Islamabad
Kashmir
Lahore
PAKISTAN
Indus
Karachi
Hyderābād
Delhi
Kānpur
Lucknow
Patna
Ganga
Kathmandu
NEPAL
Thimbu
BHUTAN
Brahmaputra
Lhasa
TIBET
Ahmadābād
INDIA
Jabalpur
Nāgpur
Godavari
Bombay
Hyderabad
Krishna
Bangalore
Madras
Madurai
SRI LANKA
Colombo
Kandy
Calcutta
BANGLA DESH
Dhaka
Chittagong
Mandalay
Imphal
BURMA
Irrawaddy
Rangoon
Moulmein
Hanoi
Haiphong
Guiyang
Kunming
LAOS
Vientiane
Chiang Mai
THAILAND
Bangkok
CAMBODIA (KAMPUCHEA)
Phnom Penh
Ho Chi Minh
VIETNAM
Mekong
Surat Thani
George Town
Kuala Lumpur
SINGAPORE
MALAY
SUMATRA
Padang
Palemba
Jakarta

Andaman Is (Ind.)
Nicobar Is (Ind.)
Bay of Bengal
ARABIAN SEA
INDIAN OCEAN
Cocos Is (Aust.)

7
8
9
10
11
12
13
14

7 The Taj Mahal, India

8 Mount Everest, Nepal

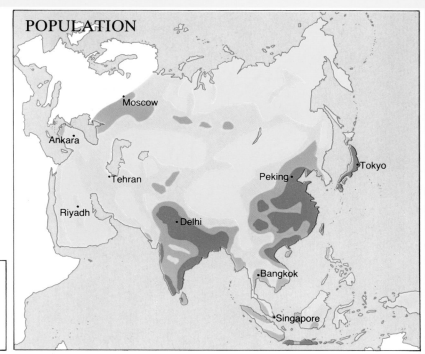

POPULATION

- over 500 persons per km²
- 100-500 persons per km²
- 5-100 persons per km²
- under 5 persons per km²

	Cattle		Oil
	Citrus fruit		Barley
	Coconut		Wheat
	Cotton		Minerals
	Fish	3	Copper
	Rice	4	Gold
	Rubber	5	Iron
	Spices	6	Lead
	Tea	7	Nickel
	Timber	11	Uranium
	Coal	12	Zinc

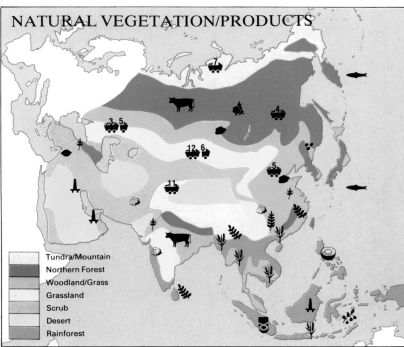

NATURAL VEGETATION/PRODUCTS

- Tundra/Mountain
- Northern Forest
- Woodland/Grass
- Grassland
- Scrub
- Desert
- Rainforest

DID YOU KNOW THAT …?

1 The world's heaviest bell is the *Czar Bell* in Moscow's Kremlin. It weighs a massive 196 tonnes (193 tons) and is 5.87 m (19 ft 3 in) high! The bell was cast in 1735. It is now cracked, and hasn't been rung since 1836.

2 In Siberia, USSR, there is a huge forest called the *taiga*, which makes up a quarter of the total area of forest in the world! The trees are mostly evergreens – pine and larch. Few people used to live in the taiga, as it is a very cold area, but because it is rich in minerals more people are moving into the forest. They live in industrial towns being built deep in its heart, to exploit the minerals.

3 The huge Gobi Desert covers much of Mongolia. The Gobi is a cold, barren region of rocky plains and hills. Water is very scarce and only a few nomads live here. They exist mainly by cattle raising and live in an unusual tent called a *yurt*, which is shaped like an upside-down bowl.

4 The Great Wall of China stretches for 3460 km (2150 miles), making it the longest in the world. It was built for defence in the 3rd century BC and kept in good repair until 400 years ago. Although part of the wall was blown up to make a dam in 1979, the many remaining sections of the wall are still impressive.

11 Floating vegetable market, Thailand

14 Singapore

12 Bangkok, Thailand

5 Cliff dwellings in Cappadocia, Turkey

13 Water buffalo ploughing Chinese paddy fields

DID YOU KNOW THAT ...?

5 In central Turkey, near Urgup in the region called Cappadocia, an extraordinary landscape can be seen. There was once a plateau here, made up of layers of rock, some hard and some much softer. Over thousands of years the softer rocks have been eroded by the weather, by streams and even by men digging out caves to live in. The rocks are now shaped into strange cones, towers and 'mushrooms', with 'hats' of harder rock balancing on top! There are also complete 'villages' of caves connected to each other by passageways cut through the rock. Each cave has 'cupboards' and 'shelves' cut into its walls. Here many centuries ago people hid from religious persecution. Over 300 churches which they dug out of the rock have been found. Some people still live in caves in this region, today.

6 The Seikan Tunnel in Japan is the longest tunnel in the world! It is an underwater tunnel, stretching for 54 km (34 miles). It was built for Japan's famous *bullet train*, the first passenger train to travel at 200 kph.

7 There should have been two Taj Mahals in India – a black one and a white one! In 1648, Emperor Shah Jahan completed the present Taj Mahal. It was a tomb for his wife, and made of white marble. He then began building a tomb of black marble for himself. Before work had got very far, he was overthrown.

8 At 8848 m (29 028 ft) the peak of Mt Everest in the Himalayas is the Earth's highest point! In May 1953, New Zealander Sir Edmund Hillary was the first man to climb Everest. Twenty two years later, in 1975, the first woman to reach the summit was Junko Tabei of Japan.

9 In India cows are sacred animals and are allowed to wander freely, even in the centre of big cities! Drivers are used to going round cows lying peacefully in the middle of the road.

10 Banyan trees can be seen in India and Sri Lanka. They are very unusual to look at, because what seems to be several trees growing close together, is actually just one tree! Aerial roots grow down from the banyan's branches and root in the ground. They become extra 'trunks' and support a huge canopy of leaves, which gives a lot of shade, very useful in such a hot climate.

11 Throughout Asia there a areas where many people live boats – because there is not enoug room for them to live in houses land (or they cannot afford to) because they just prefer to live water. In these places, even t shops are on boats!

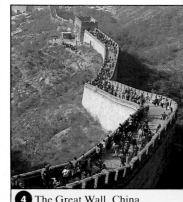

4 The Great Wall, China

Banyan tree, India

Street in India

Bangkok, Thailand, once had many canals, called *klongs*, in-[ste]ad of roads. (The city was called 'Venice of the East' because [the] klongs reminded visitors of the [can]als in Venice, Italy.) They were [use]d for transport and also helped [to] drain the land during the rainy [sea]son. After cars and lorries be-[gan] to be used for transport, many [of] the klongs were filled in to make [roa]ds. Now Bangkok has problems [wit]h flooding when the monsoons [co]me.

Paddy fields, the irrigated [ ] fields in which rice is grown, [get] their name from *padi*, the [Ma]layan word for rice. Rice is [gr]own throughout Asia in the fer-[tile] lowlands near the equator. [Mi]llions of people live in these [are]as, and rice is very important to [th]em as it yields more food per acre [tha]n any other crop.

Over half the population of the [ ] world lives in Asia – that is [2 8]82 000 000 people! Some parts [of] Asia have many people living in [a] small area. One of the most [de]nsely populated countries is [Sin]gapore, which has an average of [43]39 people for each square [kil]ometre of ground!

AFGHANISTAN

Area: 674 500 sq km (260 424 sq miles)
Population: 14 400 000
Capital: Kabul
Languages: Pashtu, Dari, Uzbek
Currency: Afghani

INDONESIA

Area: 1 919 263 sq km (741 027 miles)
Population: 161 600 000
Capital: Jakarta
Language: Bahasa (Indonesian)
Currency: Rupiah

ISRAEL

Area: 20 770 sq km (8019 sq miles)
Population: 4 200 000
Capital: Jerusalem
Languages: Hebrew, Arabic
Currency: Shekel

PAKISTAN

Area: 803 941 sq km (310 402 sq miles)
Population: 97 300 000
Capital: Islamabad
Language: Urdu
Currency: Pakistan Rupee

THAILAND

Area: 513 517 sq km (198 269 sq miles)
Population: 51 700 000
Capital: Bangkok
Languages: Thai, Chinese
Currency: Baht

CHINA

Area: 9 561 000 sq km (3 691 502 sq miles)
Population: 1 034 500 000
Capital: Peking
Language: Chinese (Mandarin)
Currency: Yuan

IRAN

Area: 1 648 184 sq km (636 364 sq miles)
Population: 43 800 000
Capital: Tehran
Language: Persian (Farsi)
Currency: Rial

JAPAN

Area: 371 000 sq km (143 243 sq miles)
Population: 119 900 000
Capital: Tokyo
Language: Japanese
Currency: Yen

SAUDI ARABIA

Area: 2 400 930 sq km (927 000 sq miles)
Population: 10 800 000
Capital: Riyadh
Language: Arabic
Currency: Riyal

TURKEY

Area: 780 576 sq km (301 380 sq miles)
Population: 50 200 000
Capital: Ankara
Language: Turkish
Currency: Turkish Lira

INDIA

Area: 3 287 593 sq km (1 269 340 sq miles)
Population: 746 400 000
Capital: Delhi
Languages: Hindi, English
Currency: Indian Rupee

IRAQ

Area: 434 924 sq km (167 924 sq miles)
Population: 15 000 000
Capital: Baghdad
Language: Arabic
Currency: Iraqi Dinar

MALAYSIA

Area: 330 669 sq km (127 671 sq miles)
Population: 15 300 000
Capital: Kuala Lumpur
Language: Malay
Currency: Ringgit (Malaysian Dollar)

SINGAPORE

Area: 616 sq km (238 sq miles)
Population: 2 500 000
Capital: Singapore
Languages: Chinese, Malay, Tamil, English
Currency: Singapore Dollar

USSR

Area: 22 402 000 sq km (8 649 412 sq miles)
Population: 274 000 000
Capital: Moscow
Language: Russian
Currency: Ruble

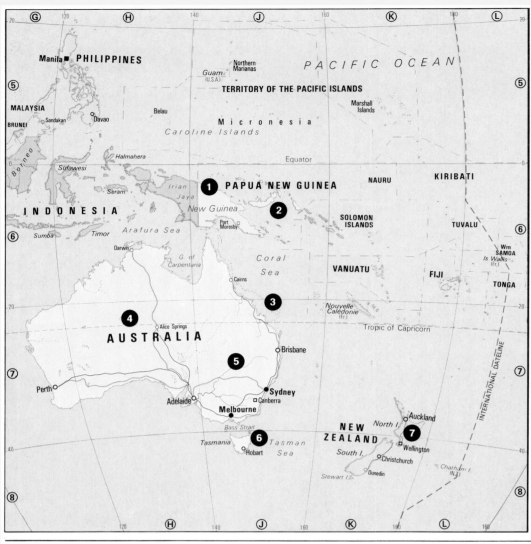

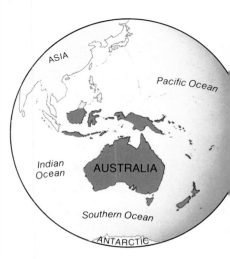

7 Geysers at Whakarewarewa, New Zealand

DID YOU KNOW THAT ...?

1 Over 700 languages are spoken in Papua New Guinea! That is more than a quarter of all the languages spoken in the world! Papua New Guinea's mountains, thick forests and islands meant that different tribes did not mix, so they did not share a common language, but instead each developed its own. Today, Pidgin English and Police Motu have become the languages which the different tribes use to talk to each other.

2 No less than 38 different species of the beautiful Bird of Paradise are to be seen in Papua New Guinea! Another 5 species are found on neighbouring islands and in northern Australia. Their tail feathers are a traditional part of Papua New Guinea tribal costume, although the birds are now protected from hunting to a great extent.

3 Australia's Great Barrier Reef is formed from the shells of millions of tiny sea creatures! It is 2000 km (1250 miles) long and is the world's biggest coral reef. There are many thousands of coral islands or *atolls* in the Pacific region.

4 Ayers Rock is a huge sand-stone rock formation which rears up abruptly from the desert in central Australia. The rock is special because it changes colour with the light. Australia's native *aborigine* people believe there is something magical about the rock.

5 Australia is the driest of all the continents in the world! Rainfall is also very unevenly distributed: even though the tropical north has about 2000 mm (79 inches) a year, the central deserts have less than 150 mm (6 inches). Irrigation is important for agriculture, and rivers and artesian wells are used as a source of water. The Snowy Mountains reservoir and irrigation scheme has brought water from the mountains to irrigate farmland in the eastern Australia.

6 A Tasmanian Devil is a little bear-like creature found only in Tasmania. It is just 60 cm (2 ft) long, with a big bushy tail. It has very sharp teeth and eats other

4 Ayers Rock, Australia

6 Tasmanian Devil

POPULATION

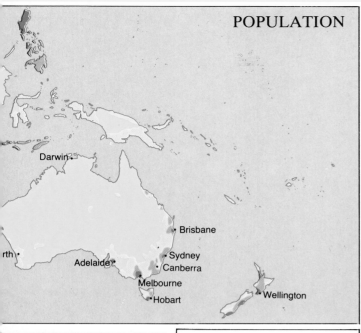

NATURAL VEGETATION/PRODUCTS

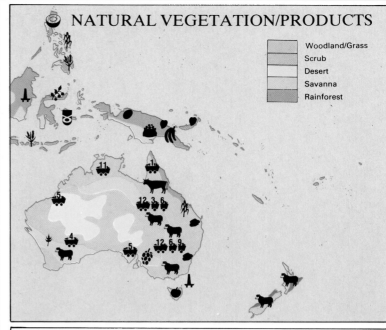

Woodland/Grass
Scrub
Desert
Savanna
Rainforest

| over 500 persons per km² |
| 100-500 persons per km² |
| 5-100 persons per km² |
| under 5 persons per km² |

Sheep
Apples
Bananas
Grapes
Coconut

Coffee
Cocoa
Rubber
Yams
Rice

Coal
Oil
Spices
Sugar cane
Wheat

Minerals
1 Bauxite
3 Copper
4 Gold
5 Iron

6 Lead
9 Silver
11 Uranium
12 Zinc

Traditional dress,
Papua New Guinea

...nals and small birds when it ...es out at night. The Tasmanian ...vil is a *marsupial*. This means it ...ries its young in a pouch.

...The tallest geyser ever to have ...erupted was the Waimangu ...yser in New Zealand. In 1904 it ...e to a height of 457 m (1500 ft). ...st erupted in 1917, killing four ...ple! Today, steam from New ...land's hot springs and geysers is ...nessed to generate electricity.

The Great Barrier Reef, Australia

AUSTRALIA

Area: 7 682 300 sq km
(2 966 136 sq miles)
Population: 15 500 000
Capital: Canberra
Language: English
Currency: Australian Dollar

NEW ZEALAND

Area: 268 675 sq km
(103 735 sq miles)
Population: 3 200 000
Capital: Wellington
Language: English
Currency: New Zealand
Dollar

TONGA

Area: 699 sq km
(270 sq miles)
Population: 97 000
Capital: Nuku'alofa
Languages: English,
Tongan
Currency: Pa'anga

FIJI

Area: 18 272 sq km
(7055 sq miles)
Population: 700 000
Capital: Suva
Languages: English, Fijian
Currency: Fiji Dollar

PAPUA NEW GUINEA

Area: 461 692 sq km
(178 259 sq miles)
Population: 3 400 000
Capital: Port Moresby
Languages: English,
Melanesian Pidgin
Currency: Kina

VANUATU

Area: 14 763 sq km
(5700 sq miles)
Population: 100 000
Capital: Vila
Languages: Bislama,
English, French
Currency: Australian Dollar,
Vatu

KIRIBATI

Area: 800 sq km
(309 sq miles)
Population: 59 000
Capital: Tarawa
Languages: English,
I Kiribati
Currency: Australian Dollar

SOLOMON ISLANDS

Area: 29 785 sq km
(11 500 sq miles)
Population: 300 000
Capital: Honiara
Languages: English, Pidgin
Currency: Solomon Islands
Dollar

WESTERN SAMOA

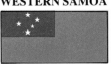

Area: 2831 sq km
(1093 sq miles)
Population: 200 000
Capital: Apia
Languages: Samoan, English
Currency: Tala

1:20M

200 400 600 800 km
200 400 mls

Glasgow
SCOTLAND
U.K.
NORTH SEA
DENMARK
Copenhagen (København)
Hamburg
GERMANY W. E.
Berlin
POLAND
Poznań
Łotódź
Wrocław
Kraków
Warsaw (Warszawa)
Carpathian Mts
Lvov
UKRAINSKAYA S.S.R.
MOLDAVSKAYA S.S.R.
Krivoy Rog
Odessa
Sevastopol'
BLACK SEA
Novorossiysk
Krasnodar
Maykop
TURKEY
Yerevan
ARMYANSKAYA S.S.R.
Tbilisi
GRUZINSKAYA S.S.R.
Tabriz
IRAN
IRAQ
Tehrān
Baku
AZERBAYDZHANSKAYA S.S.R.
Dagestanskaya A.S.S.R.

NORWEGIAN SEA
Arctic Circle
NORWAY
SWEDEN
FINLAND
Lappland
BALTIC SEA
Stockholm
ESTONSKAYA S.S.R.
Helsinki
Novgorod
LATVIYSKAYA S.S.R.
Riga
LITOVSKAYA S.S.R.
BELORUSSKAYA S.S.R.
Minsk
Leningrad
Petrozavodsk
Kareľskaya A.S.S.R.
White Sea Beloye More
Murmansk
Koľskiy Poluostrov
Nordkapp
Arkhangeľsk
Moscow (Moskva)
Smolensk
Dnepr
Bryansk
Tula
Kiyev
Kharʹkov
Dnepropetrovsk
Donetsk
Zaporozhʹye
Rostov-na-Donu
Kaloma
Yaroslavľ
Vologda
Voronezh
Saratov
Kuybyshev
Volgograd
Kalmytskaya A.S.S.R.
Astrakhanʹ
Volga
CASPIAN SEA
Mordovskaya A.S.S.R.
Gorʹkiy 1
Mariyskaya A.S.S.R.
Kazan
Tatarskaya A.S.S.R.
Udmurtskaya A.S.S.R.
Izhevsk
Perm'
Ufa
Bashkirskaya A.S.S.R.
Magnitogorsk
Uraľsk
Aktyubinsk

BARENTS SEA
SPITSBERGEN (Nor.)
NOVAYA ZEMLYA
KARA SEA
Gydanskiy Poluostrov
FRANZ-JOSEF-LAND
ARCTIC
Vorkuta
Komi A.S.S.R.
Syktyvkar
Kirov
ROSSIYS
Zapadno
Sibirskaya
Nizmennost
Sverdlovsk
Chelyabinsk
Ob'
Omsk
Novosibirsk
Tomsk
Novokuzn
Barn
Ob'
Kokchetav
Semipalatinsk
Karaganda
KAZAKHSKAYA S.S.R.
Araľskoye More
Kara-Kalpakskaya A.S.S.R.
Kzyl Orda
Ozero Balkhash
TURKMENSKAYA S.S.R.
UZBEKSKAYA S.S.R.
Tashkent
Alma Ata
KIRGIZSKAYA S.S.R.
Tien Shan
Pik Pobedy 7439
Leninabad
Karshi
TADZHIKSKAYA S.S.R.
Pik Kommunizma
Pamir
AFGHANISTAN
SINK

R.S.F.S.R.

1 Chuvashkaya A.S.S.R.
2 Checheno-Ingushskaya A.S.S.R.
3 Severo-Osetinskaya A.S.S.R.
4 Kabardino-Balkarskaya A.S.S.R.

GRUZINSKAYA S.S.R.

5 Abkhazskaya A.S.S.R.
6 Adzharskaya A.S.S.R.

AZERBAYDZHANSKAYA S.S.R.

7 Nakhichevanskaya A.S.S.R.

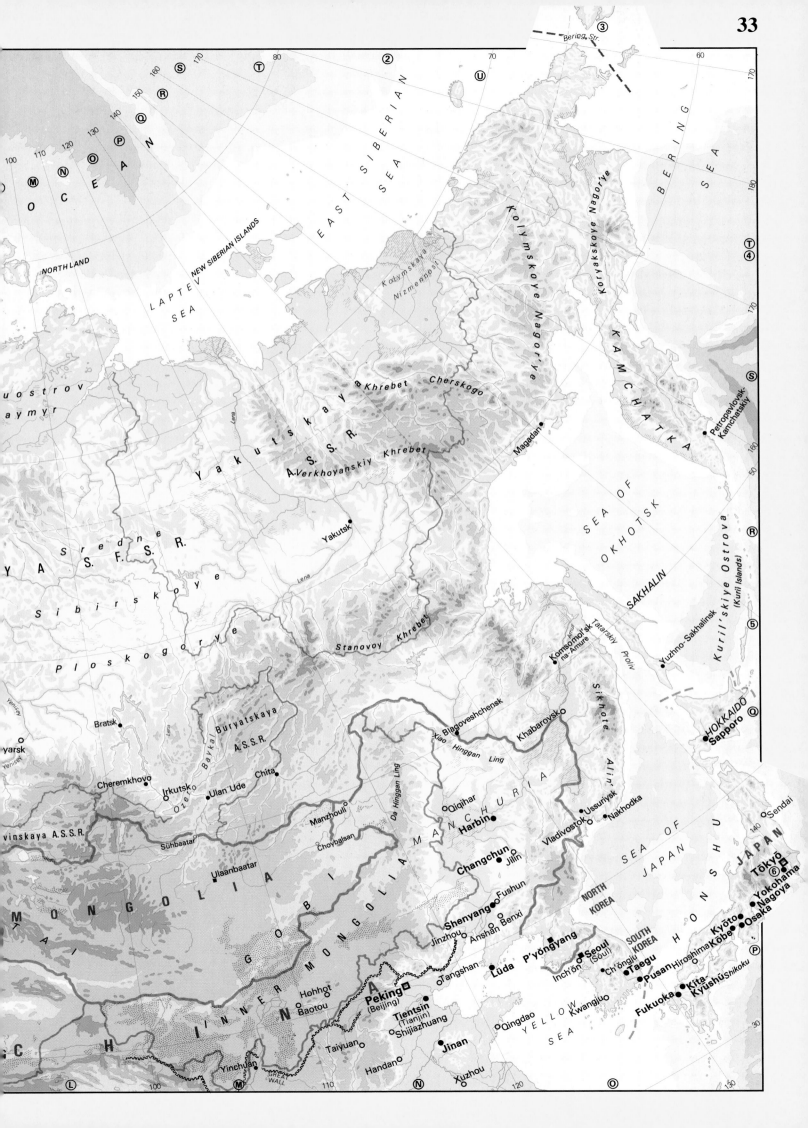

① Bering Str.

NORTH LAND

EAST SIBERIAN SEA

NEW SIBERIAN ISLANDS

LAPTEV SEA

ostrov aymyr

Kolymskaya Nizmennost

KAMCHATKA

Kolyvakskoye Nagor'ye

Kolymskoye Nagor'ye

BERING SEA

Yakutskay A.S.S.R.

Khrebet Cherskogo

Lena

Verkhoyanskiy Khrebet

Petropavlovsk-Kamchatskiy

Magadan

Yakutsk

SEA OF OKHOTSK

R.S.F.S.R.

Sredne Sibirskoye Ploskogor'ye

Lena

SAKHALIN

Kuril'skiye Ostrova (Kuril Islands)

Stanovoy Khrebet

Bratsk

yarsk

Yenisey

Yenisey

Cheremkhovo

Bayla Buryatskaya A.S.S.R.

Irkutsk

Ozero Baykal

Ulan Ude

Chita

Komsomol'sk na-Amure

Tatarskiy Proliv

Yuzhno-Sakhalinsk

Khabarovsko

Sikhote Alin'

HOKKAIDŌ Sapporo

Blagoveshchensk

Xiao Hinggan Ling

vinskaya A.S.S.R.

Manzhouli

Sühbaatar

Choybalsan

Da Hinggan Ling

MANCHURIA

Qiqihar

Harbin

Ussuriysk

Nakhodka

Vladivostok

SEA OF JAPAN

Sendai

Ulaanbaatar

MONGOLIA

GOBI

Changchun

Jilin

Fushun

NORTH KOREA

HONSHU

JAPAN

Tōkyō ⑥

Yokohama

Nagoya

Shenyang

Anshan Benxi

Jinzhou

P'yŏngyang

Seoul (Sŏul)

SOUTH KOREA

Kyōto

Kōbe Osaka

MONGOLIA

INNER MONGOLIA

Hohhot

Baotou

Peking (Beijing)

Tangshan

Lüda

Inch'ŏn

Ch'ŏngju

Taegu

Pusan

Hiroshima Kita Kyūshū Shikoku

Fukuoka

C H I N A

Tientsin (Tianjin)

Shijiazhuang

Taiyuan

Handan

Yinchuan

GREAT WALL

Jinan

Qingdao

YELLOW SEA

Kwangju

Xuzhou

② ③ ⑤ ⑥ Ⓢ Ⓣ Ⓡ Ⓠ Ⓟ Ⓞ Ⓝ Ⓜ Ⓛ ④ U

1:20M

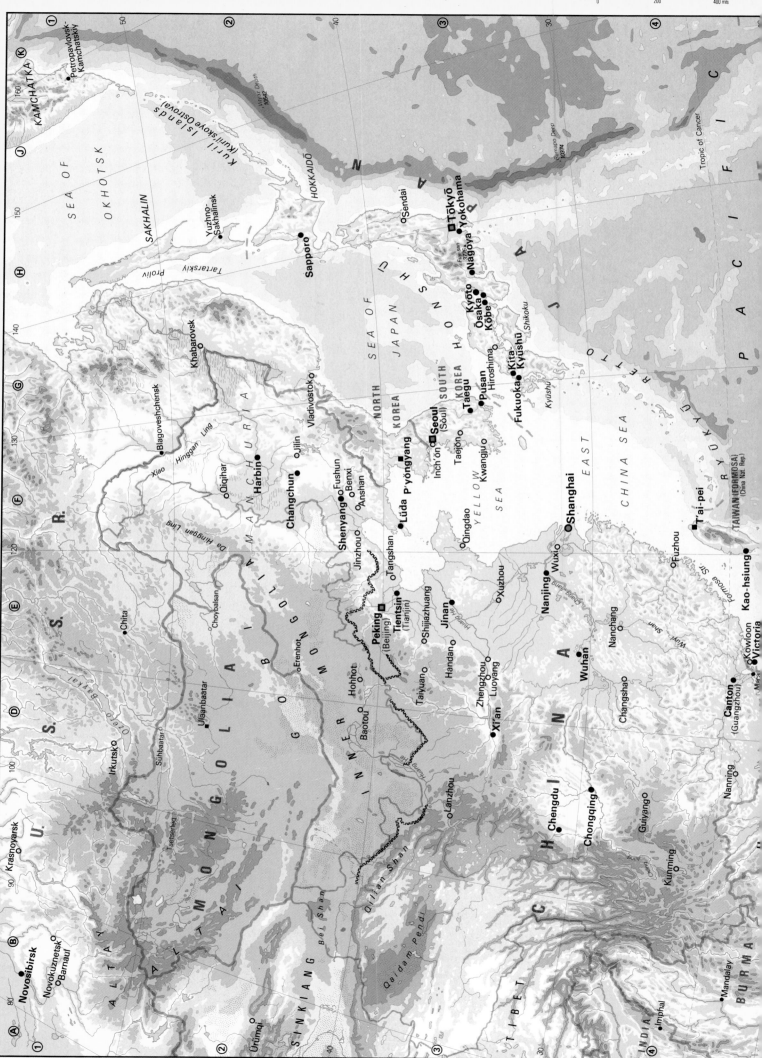

200   400   600   800 km
200   400 mls

KAMCHATKA

Petropavlovsk-Kamchatskiy

SEA OF OKHOTSK

Kuril'skiye Ostrova)
Kuril Islands

Vityaz Deep 10542

SAKHALIN

Proliv Tatarskiy

Yuzhno-Sakhalinsk

HOKKAIDŌ

Sapporo

Sendai

Tōkyō
Yokohama

Fuji-san 3776

Nagoya
Kyōto
Ōsaka
Kōbe

Hiroshima

Kita-
Kyūshū
Fukuoka

Kyūshū   Shikoku

Khabarovsk

Blagoveshchensk

Xiao Hinggan Ling

MANCHURIA

Harbin

Changchun

Jilin

Qiqihar

Fushun
Benxi
Shenyang   Anshan

Vladivostok

NORTH KOREA

P'yŏngyang

Lüda

SEA OF JAPAN

SOUTH KOREA

Seoul
(Sŏul)

Inch'ŏn

Taejŏn
Kwangju

Taegu
Pusan

EAST CHINA SEA

Da Hinggan Ling

Jinzhou

Tangshan

Peking
(Beijing)

Tientsin
(Tianjin)

Shijiazhuang

Qingdao

Jinan

Handan

Taiyuan

Hohhot

Baotou

Erenhot

Choybalsan

Ulaanbaatar

Sühbaatar

Tsetserleg

Irkutsk

Chita

Krasnoyarsk

Novosibirsk
Novokuznetsk
Barnaul

ALTAY

SINKIANG

Ürümqi

Bēi Shan

Qilian Shan

Qaidam Pendi

TIBET

BURMA

INDIA

Imphal

Mandalay

Kunming

Nanning

Guiyang

Chongqing

Chengdu

CHINA

Xi'an

Zhengzhou
Luoyang

Xuzhou

Nanjing

Wuxi

Shanghai

Wuhan

Nanchang

Changsha

Canton
(Guangzhou)

Macau

Kowloon
Victoria

Kao-hsiung

T'ai-pei

TAIWAN (FORMOSA)
(China Nat. Rep.)

Fuzhou

Formosa Str.

Tropic of Cancer

PACIFIC OCEAN

RYUKYU RETTO

YELLOW SEA

Huang He

Chang Jiang

Wu Shan

Lanzhou

MONGOLIA

INNER MONGOLIA

GOBI

U.S.S.R.

Ozero Baykal

R.

Tomano Deep 10374

NANSEI

Kyūshū

Kunming

1:10M

100 | 200 | 300 | 400 km
100 | 200 mls

Ⓐ 100 Ⓐ 105 Ⓑ 110 Ⓒ 115 Ⓓ 120 Ⓔ

M O N G O L I A

G O B I

Chang J

①

Y i n n S h a n

Shenyang ●

INNER **MONGOLIA**

Y i n *Shan*

Hohhot ○

Jinzhou ○   Anshan ●

Baotou ○

L i a o n i n g

40

GREAT WALL

Peking (Beijing) ■

Tangshan ○

②

Shan

Hebei

Tientsin (Tianjin) ●

Dairen (Lüda) ●

BO HAI

Ningxia

Taiyuan ○

Shanxi

Shijiazhuang ○

Qinghai

Lülliang Shan

Taihang Shan

Tsinan (Jinan) ●

Lanzhou ○

Huang He

Handan ○

S h a n d o n g

Huang He

Tsingtao (Qingdao) ○

35

YELLOW

Shaanxi

Luoyang ○

Zhengzhou ○

H e n a n

Xuzhou ○

Sian (Xi'an) ●

Qin Ling

Huang He

Huang He

③

C **H** **I** **N** **A**

Daba Shan

Jiangsu

A n h u i

Nanking (Nanjing) ●

Wuxi ○
Suzhou ○

Sha

Chengdu ●

H u b e i

Dabie Shan

Tai Hu

Daxue Shan

S i c h u a n

Chang Jiang

Wuhan ●

Chang Jiang

Hangzhou ○

30

Chungking (Chongqing) ●

Mufu Shan

Poyang Hu

Z h e j i a n g

Wuling Shan

Nanchang ○

Dalou Shan

Changsha ○

J i a n g x i

④

G u i z h o u

H u n a n

Luoxiao Shan

F u j i a n

Guiyang ○

Foochow (Fuzhou) ○

STRAIT

FORMOSA

25

Kunming ○

Nan Ling

T'ai

Y u n n a n

T A I W

G u a n g x i

G u a n g d o n g

Kao-hsiung ●

Canton (Guangzhou) ●

⑤

Nanning ○

Kowloon ○
Victoria

VIETNAM

Macau ○
(Port.)   **HONG KONG** (U.K.)

LAOS

S O U T H

Hanoi ■

C H I N A   *S E A*

20

Ⓐ 105 Ⓑ 110 Ⓒ 115 Ⓓ 120

HAINAN DAO
110

1:10M

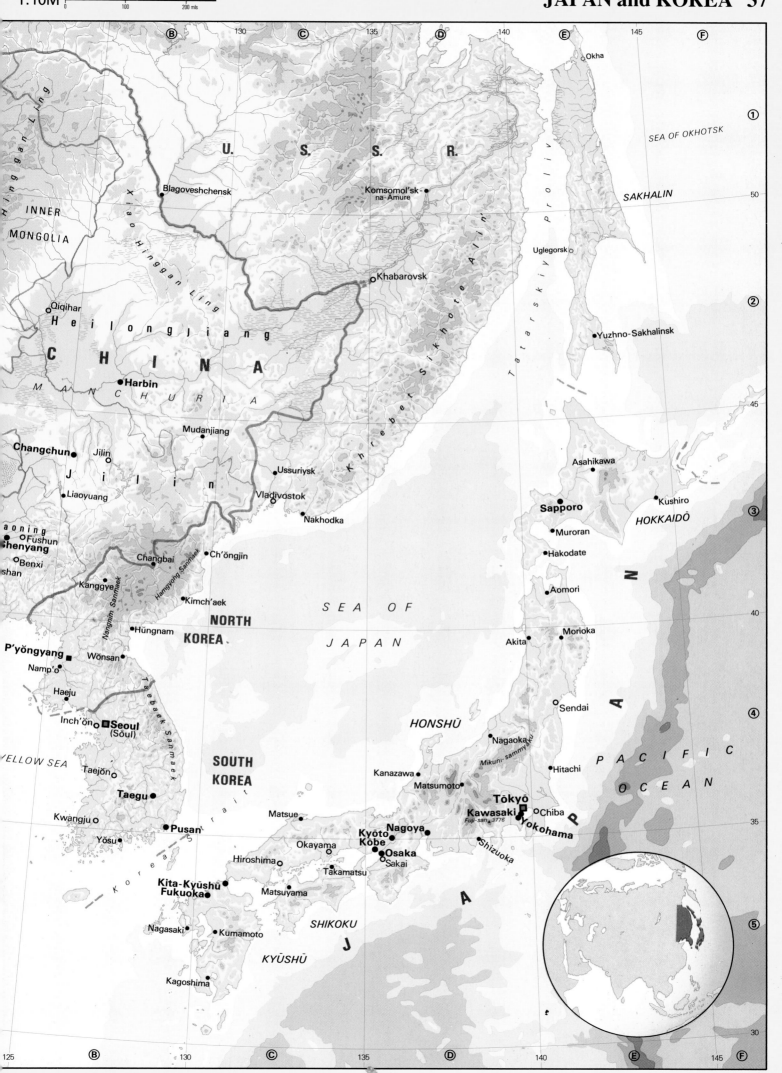

0   100   200   300   400 km
0   100   200 mls

Ⓑ   130   Ⓒ   135   Ⓓ   140   Ⓔ   145   Ⓕ

Okha

SEA OF OKHOTSK

①

50

Blagoveshchensk

Komsomol'sk-
na-Amure

SAKHALIN

U.   S.   S.   R.

INNER
MONGOLIA

Xiao Hinggan Ling

Hinggan Ling

Qiqihar

Heilongjiang

CHINA

Harbin

MANCHURIA

Khabarovsk

Uglegorsk

②

Yuzhno-Sakhalinsk

45

Mudanjiang

Changchun   Jilin

J i l i n

Liaoyuang

Ussuriysk

Vladivostok

Nakhodka

Asahikawa

Kushiro

Sapporo

HOKKAIDŌ

③

aoning
Fushun
henyang

Benxi
shan

Changbai

Ch'ŏngjin

Kanggye

Kimch'aek

Muroran

Hakodate

Aomori

N

Khrebet Sikhote Alin'

Tatarskiy Proliv

Hamgyong Sanmaek

Nangnim Sanmaek

NORTH
KOREA

SEA   OF

JAPAN

Morioka

Akita

40

Hüngnam

P'yŏngyang   Wŏnsan

Namp'o

Haeju

Taebaek Sanmaek

Inch'ŏn Seoul
(Sŏul)

SOUTH
KOREA

Sendai

④

HONSHŪ

Nagaoka

Mikuni-sammyaku

Hitachi

PACIFIC

Taejŏn

Taegu

Kwangju

Pusan

Yŏsu

Kanazawa

Matsumoto

Matsue

Okayama

Hiroshima

Kyōto
Kōbe
Osaka
Sakai

Nagoya

Tōkyō
Kawasaki
Fuji-san 3776
Yokohama

Chiba

Shizuoka

OCEAN

35

YELLOW SEA

Korea Strait

Kita-Kyūshū
Fukuoka

Matsuyama

Takamatsu

SHIKOKU

J

A

P

Nagasaki   Kumamoto

KYŪSHŪ

Kagoshima

⑤

125   Ⓑ   130   Ⓒ   135   Ⓓ   140   Ⓔ   145   Ⓕ

30

1:20M

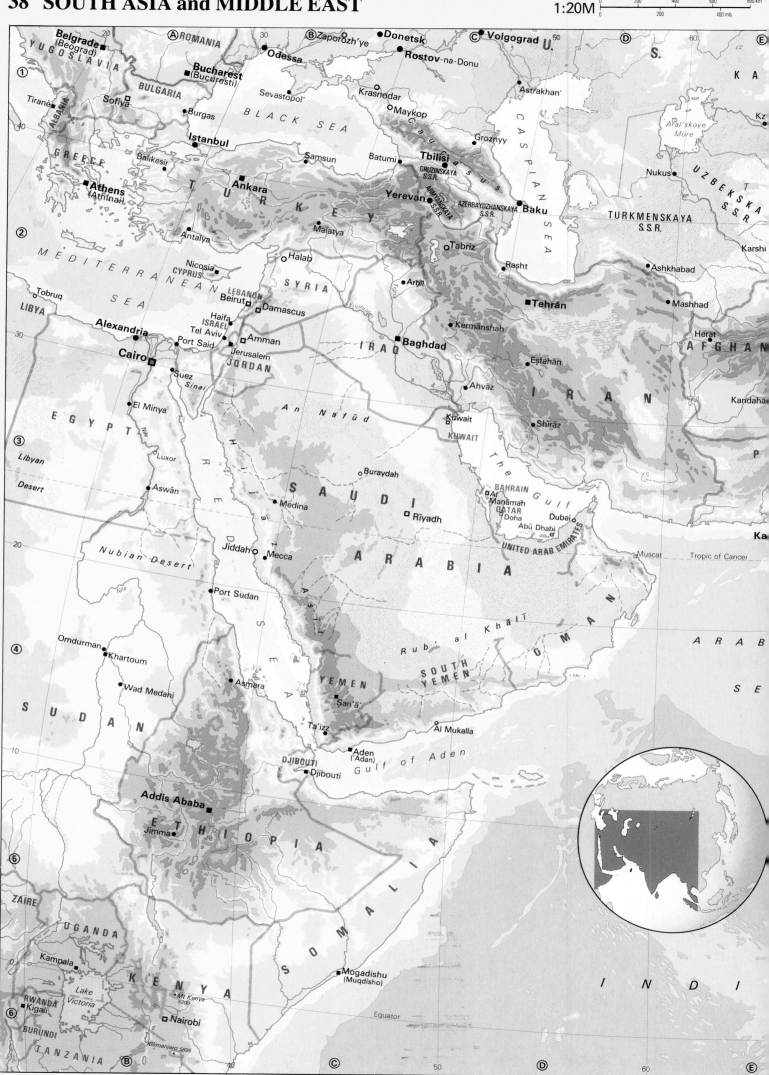

200 400 600 800 km
200 400 mls

Ⓐ ROMANIA
Belgrade (Beograd)
YUGOSLAVIA
20
Zaporozh'ye Ⓑ
Donetsk
Volgograd Ⓒ U.
50 Ⓓ 60 Ⓔ
Bucharest (Bucureşti)
Odessa
Rostov-na-Donu
K A
①
Tiranë
ALBANIA
Sofiya
BULGARIA
Burgas
Sevastopol'
Krasnodar
Maykop
Astrakhan'
C A S P I A N
Aral'skoye More
Kz
40
B L A C K   S E A
Caucasus
Groznyy
Kz
GREECE
Istanbul
Balıkesir
Samsun
Batumi
Tbilisi
GRUZINSKAYA S.S.R.
Nukus
UZBEKSKA
Athens (Athínai)
T U R
Ankara
K E Y
Malatya
Yerevan
ARMYANSKAYA S.S.R.
AZERBAYDZHANSKAYA S.S.R.
Baku
S E A
TURKMENSKAYA S.S.R.
②
Antalya
Halab
S Y R I A
Tabriz
Rasht
Ashkhabad
Karshi
M E D I T E R R A N E A N
Nicosia
CYPRUS
Beirut
LEBANON
Damascus
Tigris
Arbil
Euphrates
Tehrān
Mashhad
S E A
Tobruq
Haifa
ISRAEL
Tel Aviv
Amman
Jerusalem
JORDAN
I R A Q
Baghdad
Kermānshah
Eşfahān
Herat
AFGHAN
LIBYA
Alexandria
Cairo
Port Said
Suez
Sinai
Ahvāz
I R A N
③
El Minya
An Nafūd
Kuwait
KUWAIT
Shīrāz
Kandaha
E G Y P T
Libyan
Nile
Luxor
Aswān
Buraydah
S A U D I
BAHRAIN
Al Manāmah
QATAR
Doha
Dubai
UNITED ARAB EMIRATES
Ka
Desert
Médina
Rīyadh
Abū Dhabi
The Gulf
P
20
Nubian Desert
Jiddah
Mecca
A R A B I A
Tropic of Cancer
Muscat
R E D
Port Sudan
Rub' al Khālī
O M A N
A R A B
④
Omdurman
Khartoum
Asmara
YEMEN
SOUTH YEMEN
S E
Wad Medani
S E A
San'ā'
Al Mukalla
S U D A N
Ta'izz
Aden ('Adan)
Gulf of Aden
DJIBOUTI
Djibouti
Addis Ababa
S O M A L I A
I N D I
⑤
Jimma
E T H I O P I A
ZAIRE
UGANDA
⑥
Kampala
RWANDA
Kigali
BURUNDI
Lake Victoria
K E N Y A
Mt Kenya 5200
Nairobi
TANZANIA
Kilimanjaro 5895
Equator
Ⓑ 40
Ⓒ 50
Ⓓ 60
Ⓔ

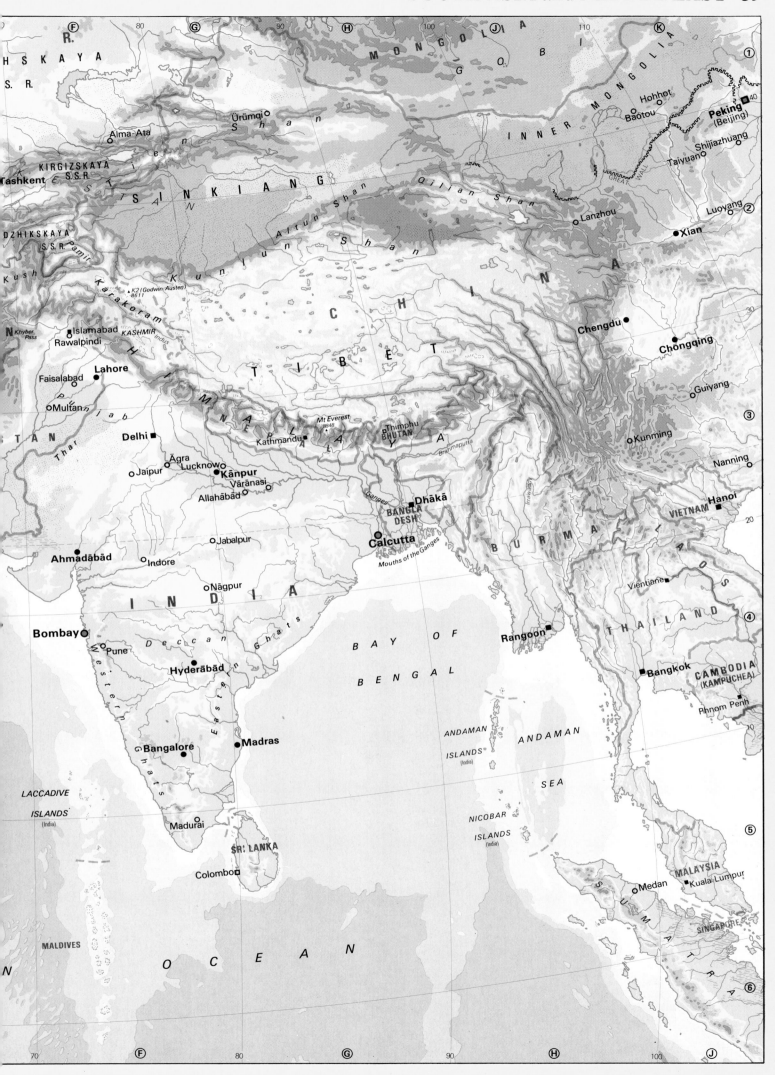

1:10M

100 200 300 400 km

100 200 mls

Ⓐ 95 Ⓑ 100 Ⓒ 105 Ⓓ 110 Ⓔ

① Lao Cai CHINA Nanning

Pingxiang

B U R M A • Mandalay Mao

• Myingyan Zhanjiang

Meiktila Hanoi ■

Taung-gyi Haiphong •

20 Gulf of

• Pyinmana Mekong Luang of

Prabang Haikou •

L Tongkin HAINAN

Chiang Mai • Vientiane Vinh Ya Xian •

Muang A Udon INDO

② • Henzada Phrae Thani O

Pegu • M.Phitsanulok S

Bassein • Rangoon ■ Hue CHINA

Moulmein • T H A I L A N D Da Nang

Ubon

Ratchathani Pakse

15 Nakhon

Ratchasima V

Tavoy • Khong I Qui Nhon

Bangkok E

Thon • Sisophon T Ban Me Da Lat

③ Buri • C A M B O D I A Thuot N Nha Trang

A N D A M A N B.Hua (K A M P U C H E A) A Cam Ranh

S E A Hin M

Mergui Kompong

Archipelago Phnom Cham

Penh ■

GULF Chau Saigon (Ho Chi Minh)

Phu My Tho

OF Vung Tau

10 THAILAND Rach Gia Can

Tho Mouths of

the Mekong

Surat

Thani

S O U T H

NICOBAR

ISLANDS C H I N A

④ (India)

S E A

5 George Kota Bharu

Town

M A L A Y S I A

Banda Aceh • Ipoh

M A L A Y A Kuala Trengganu

• Medan PENINSULAR SARAWAK

Pematangsiantar Kelang Kuala MALAYSIA (Malaysia)

⑤ Lumpur Kuching

Simeulue Melaka Singkawang

S

U Johor

M Bharu

Padangsidempuan A SINGAPORE ■

Nias T Pekanbaru • B O R N E

R Pontianak •

0 A

Equator

⑥ P.P.Batu Rengat

Padang I N D O N E S I A

Siberut Jambi •

Ⓐ 95 Ⓑ 100 Ⓒ 105 Ⓓ 110 Ⓔ

Irrawaddy

Mouths of the Irrawaddy

Strait of Malacca

1:7.5M

100   200   300 km
50   100   150 mils

Baku

Ardabīl

Tabrīz

Urumīyeh

Hamadān

Kermānshāh

Khorramābād

Ahvāz

Abādān

Basra

KUWAIT

Kuwait

Hafar al Bāṭin

An Nāṣirīyah

Yerevan

Kirovakan

Erzurum

Kirkūk

Arbīl

Mosul

Baghdād

An Najaf

U.S.S.R.

I R A N

K u r d i s t a n

Tigris

Tigris

Al Hadīthah

Ar Rutbah

Al Jālamīd

I R A Q

Badiyat ash Shām

Al Widyān

Al ʾIsawīyah

Sakākah

S A U D I   A R A B I A

Anadolu Dağları

Samsun

Sivas

Malatya

Urup

Adana

Ankara

Antalya

Balıkesir

İzmir

İstanbul

T U R K E Y

Toros Dağları

Urfa

Al Jazirah

Euphrates

S Y R I A

ʾAleppo
(Ḥalab)

Hamāh

Ḥimṣ

Al Lādhiqīyah

Tripoli

Beirut
(Beyrouth)

LEBANON

Damascus
(Dimashq)

Amman

Jerusalem

Nazareth

Haifa

Tel Avîv Yafo

Gaza

Beersheba

Negev

J O R D A N

Dead
Sea

Al
Mudawwara

Ṭabūk

ISRAEL

Nicosia

CYPRUS

M e d i t e r r a n e a n
S e a

Port Said
(Būr Saʿīd)

Suez
(El Suweis)

Gulf of Suez

Cairo
(El Qāhira)

El Gîza

Tanta

El Minya

Alexandria
(El Iskandarîya)

E G Y P T

S I N A I

Qattâra
Depression

GREECE

1:20M

200 400 600 800 km
200 400 mils

Manado
Halmahera
BORNEO
MOLUCCAS
IRIAN JAYA
Pegunungan Maoke
NEW GUINEA
PAPUA
Bismarck Archipelago
New
NEW GUINE
Balikpapan
CELEBES (SULAWESI)
INDONESIA
Banda Sea
New

Port Moresby
Arafura Sea
Torres Strait
Timor
Timor Sea
Darwin
Gulf of Carpentaria
Great Barrier R
Isla

INDIAN
OCEAN
NORTHERN
TERRITORY
QUEENSLAND
Cairns
Townsville
Mack
Great

Great Sandy Desert
Dampier
WESTERN
AUSTRALIA
AUSTRALIA
Alice Springs
Ayers Rock
Lake Eyre Basin
L. Eyre
SOUTH
Dividing
Darling

Geraldton
Kalgoorlie
Great Victoria Desert
AUSTRALIA
NEW SOUTH WALES
Ne
Sydn
Wollongon

Perth
Fremantle
Great Australian Bight
Adelaide
Murray
Murray
Canb
VICTORIA

Geelong
Melbourne
Bass Strait

Hobart
TASMA

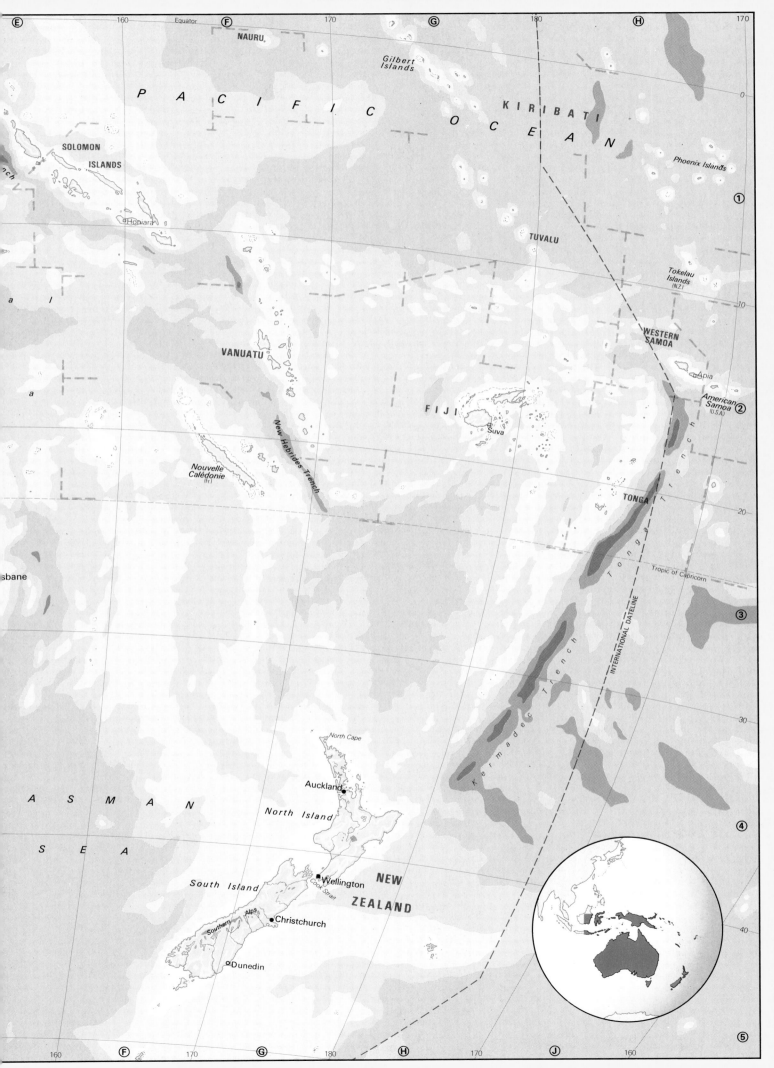

E   160   Equator   F   170   G   180   H   170

NAURU

Gilbert Islands

P A C I F I C

KIRIBATI

O C E A N

Phoenix Islands

0

SOLOMON

ISLANDS

①

□Honiara

TUVALU

Tokelau Islands (N.Z.)

10

a   l

WESTERN SAMOA

□Apia

a

VANUATU

FIJI

American Samoa (U.S.A.)

②

□Suva

Nouvelle Calédonie (Fr.)

New Hebrides Trench

TONGA

20

Tropic of Capricorn

bane

Kermadec Trench

Tonga Trench

INTERNATIONAL DATELINE

③

30

North Cape

④

A S M A N

Auckland●

North Island

S E A

NEW

South Island

Wellington■

Cook Strait

40

ZEALAND

Southern Alps

●Christchurch

□Dunedin

⑤

160   F   170   G   180   H   170   J   160

1:5M

Ⓐ 170 Ⓑ 175 Ⓒ

50 100 150 200 km
50 100 mls

North Cape

Kaikohe○

Whangarei○

Auckland○
Manukau●

Coromandel Peninsula

NORTH

ISLAND

Tauranga○
Bay of Plenty
Whakatane○

Hamilton○

Huiarau Ra.
Raukumara Ra.

Taupo○
L. Taupo

Gisborne○

New Plymouth○

Ruahine Ra.

Mt Ruapehu
2797

Hawke Bay

Napier○

Mahia Penin

S. Taranaki Bight

Wanganui○

①

T A S M A N

S E A

Palmerston N○

40

C. Farewell

Golden Bay

Tasman Bay

C O O K

Masterton○

Karamea Bight

Nelson○

S T R A I T

Wellington■

Spenser Mts

Kaikoura Ra.

Greymouth○

②

SOUTH

S O U T H E R N   *A L P S*

Pegasus Bay

ISLAND

3764
Mt Cook

Christchurch●

Canterbury Plains

Cascade Pt

Canterbury Bight

Hawkdun Ra.

Timaru○

P A C I F I C

Cromwell○

Oamaru○

45

Fiordland
Nat. Park

L. Te Anau

Manapouri○

Dunedin○

O C E A N

Invercargill○

③

F o v e a u x   S t r a i t

Stewart Island

Ⓐ 170 Ⓑ 175 Ⓒ

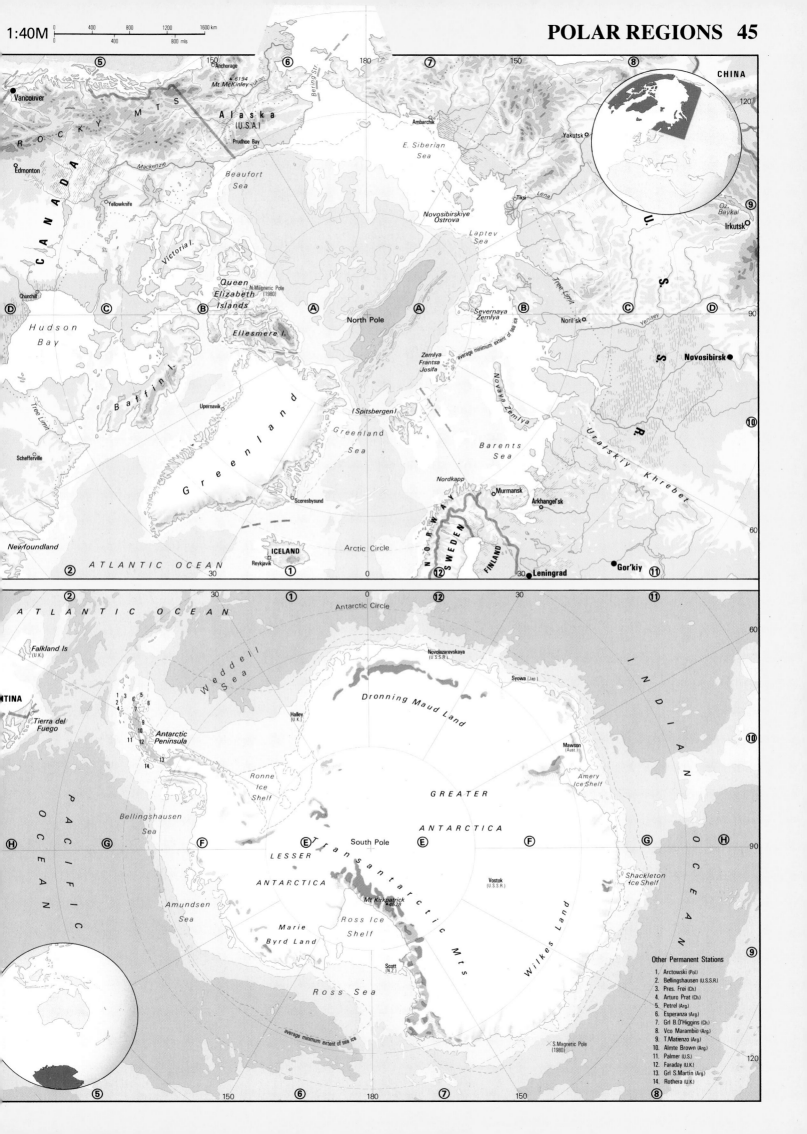

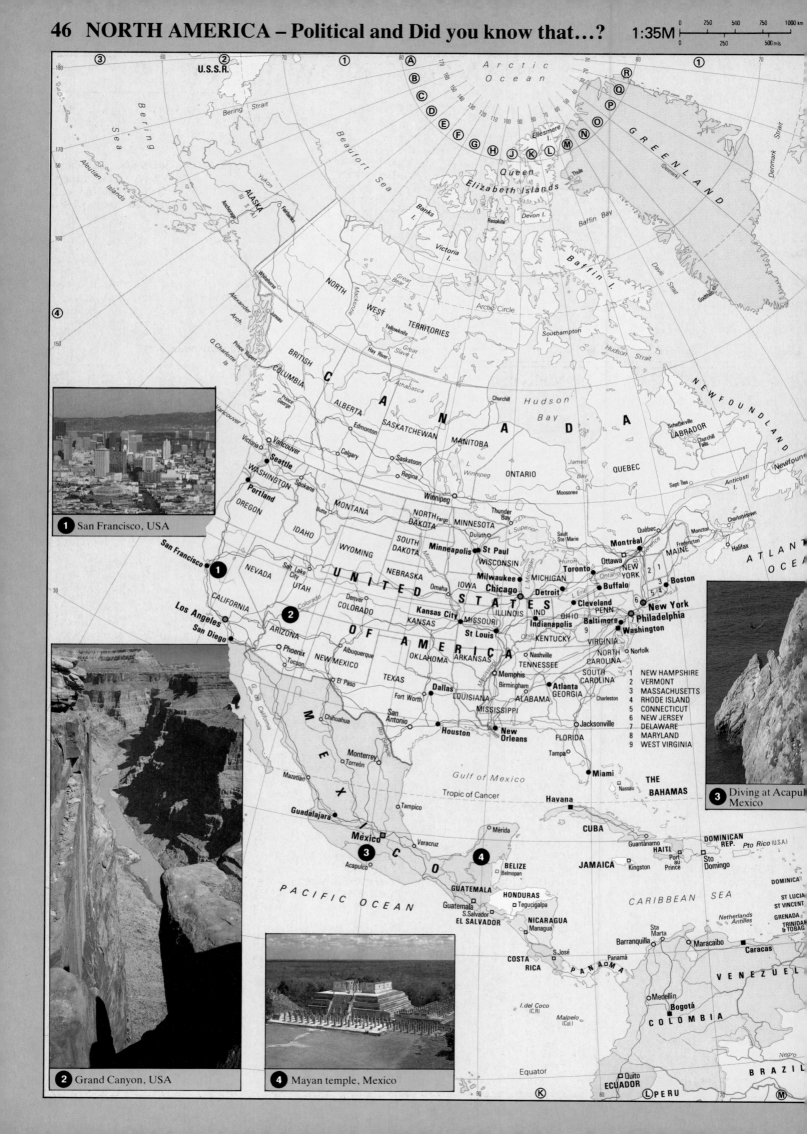

1 San Francisco, USA

2 Grand Canyon, USA

3 Diving at Acapulco, Mexico

4 Mayan temple, Mexico

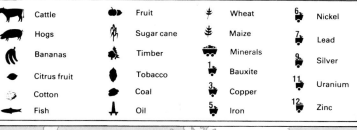

DID YOU KNOW THAT ...?

1 The city of San Francisco was almost destroyed by an earthquake in 1906, and there could be another one soon! Right under the city runs the San Andreas fault, where two of the 'plates' which make up the earth's crust slide against one another. When they get jammed together at any point, pressure builds up, until finally they break apart. This causes an earthquake because of the sudden release of so much energy. The longer the plates stay jammed together, the greater the strength of the final earthquake: in 1906, the plates under San Francisco slid 6 m (20 feet) in a few minutes! Some parts of the fault have not moved for years – and scientists think there will be another big earthquake soon.

2 The huge Grand Canyon in Arizona, USA, was gouged out of the rock by the Colorado River. It is 1.6 km (1 mile) deep, a maximum of 29 km (18 miles) wide and no less than 446 km (227 miles) long! The Grand Canyon is still being carved deeper (though very slowly) by the river.

3 At La Questrada, Acapulco, Mexico, divers often swoop 36 m (118 feet) down into the sea! This is the highest dive which people do regularly.

4 The Maya were a tribe who lived in southern Mexico and Guatemala 1400 years ago. They built great cities with stone temples, public buildings and palaces. The picture shows one of their buildings which can be seen today. It was built without help from any modern machinery!

Cattle · Hogs · Bananas · Citrus fruit · Cotton · Fish · Fruit · Sugar cane · Timber · Tobacco · Coal · Oil · Wheat · Maize · Minerals · Bauxite · Copper · Iron · 6 Nickel · 7 Lead · 9 Silver · 11 Uranium · 12 Zinc

NATURAL VEGETATION/PRODUCTS

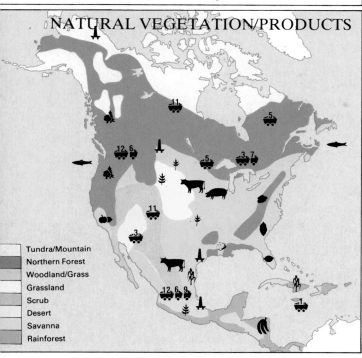

Tundra/Mountain
Northern Forest
Woodland/Grass
Grassland
Scrub
Desert
Savanna
Rainforest

POPULATION

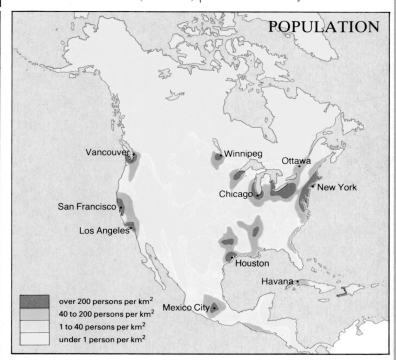

Vancouver · Winnipeg · Ottawa · Chicago · New York · San Francisco · Los Angeles · Houston · Havana · Mexico City

over 200 persons per km²
40 to 200 persons per km²
1 to 40 persons per km²
under 1 person per km²

CANADA

Area: 9 976 147 sq km (3 851 790 sq miles)
Population: 25 100 000
Capital: Ottawa
Languages: English, French
Currency: Canadian Dollar

CUBA

Area: 114 524 sq km (44 218 sq miles)
Population: 9 900 000
Capital: Havana
Language: Spanish
Currency: Cuban Peso

EL SALVADOR

Area: 20 865 sq km (8056 sq miles)
Population: 4 800 000
Capital: San Salvador
Language: Spanish
Currency: Colon

GUATEMALA
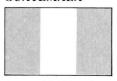
Area: 108 888 sq km (42 042 sq miles)
Population: 8 000 000
Capital: Guatemala
Language: Spanish
Currency: Quetzal

JAMAICA

Area: 11 424 sq km (4411 sq miles)
Population: 2 400 000
Capital: Kingston
Language: English
Currency: Jamaican Dollar

MEXICO

Area: 1 967 180 sq km (759 528 sq miles)
Population: 77 000 000
Capital: Mexico City
Language: Spanish
Currency: Mexican Peso

NICARAGUA

Area: 139 000 sq km (53 668 sq miles)
Population: 2 900 000
Capital: Managua
Language: Spanish
Currency: Cordoba

UNITED STATES OF AMERICA

Area: 9 363 130 sq km (3 615 104 sq miles)
Population: 236 300 000
Capital: Washington
Language: English
Currency: U.S. Dollar

1:15M

200   400   600 km
100   200   300 mls

A 170 U.S.S.R. 70 B 160 ② C 150 D 140 E 80 130 F 120 110 H

③ BERING Str. G

Bering Str.

BERING SEA

Norton Sound

ARCTIC OCEAN

BEAUFORT SEA

Barrow

Prudhoe Bay

PARRY

Banks Island

Fran Victoria Island Prince

Brooks Range

ALASKA (U.S.A.)

Yukon

Fairbanks

Alaska Range

Anchorage

Wrangell Mts.

Aleutian Ra.

Yukon

YUKON TERRITORY

Mackenzie Mountains

Paulatuk

NORTH TERRI K

Gulf of Alaska

Mackenzie

Great Bear Lake

④ 150

Whitehorse

R O C K

C

Mac

kenzie

Alexander

Yellowknife

A

Archipelago

Great Slave Lake

C O A S T

BRITISH

N

Uranium City

Peace

Queen Charlotte Islands

50

M O U N T A I N S

Skeena

Kitimat

COLUMBIA

Lake Athabasca

PACIFIC

140

Reindeer Lake

ALBERTA

SASKATCHEWAN MAN

OCEAN

Fraser

Yellowhead Pass

Edmonton

Vancouver Island

Kamloops

Kicking Horse Pass

M O U N T

Vancouver

⑤

Saskatoon

Lake Winnipe

Victoria

Calgary

Seattle

WASHINGTON

Regina

Spokane

Medicine Hat

MONTANA

Winnipeg

Portland

CASCADE RANGE

OREGON

I D A H O

A I N S

U. S.

40

Billings

NORTH DAKOTA

Nampa

SOUTH DAKOTA

A

WYOMING

S

E 130 F 120 G 110 100 H

① ⑩ Ⓚ Ⓛ

80 70 60

N
ETH
DS
NDS

Etah

Dundas

BAFFIN BAY

Baffin Island

in

ST

watin

D

HUDSON
BAY

chill

Fort Severn

Attawapiskat

Ft Rupert

Noranda

Thunder Bay

Duluth
OTA

St Paul

WISCONSIN

Madison

Milwaukee

L. MICHIGAN

L. HURON

Kitchener

Detroit

ONTARIO

LAKE SUPERIOR

Sudbury

Toronto

Hamilton

Buffalo

Ⓞ Ⓟ ② Ⓠ Ⓡ ③

80 50 40 30 20

GREENLAND

Kraulshavn

Christianshab

Arctic Circle

Angmagssalik

DENMARK STRAIT

ICELAND

Reykjavik

20

60

30

Foxe

Basin

Kekertuk

Clyde

DAVIS STRAIT

Cumberland Sound

Cape Dorset

HUDSON STRAIT

Smith I.

A

Povungnituk

Ungava
Bay

Qagssimiut

40

Labrador
Sea

④

NEWFOUNDLAND

Labrador

Cartwright

Newfoundland

50

50

Schefferville

Labrador
City

St John's

QUEBEC

Sept-Iles

Chibougamau

St Lawrence

Gulf of
Saint Lawrence

PRINCE
EDWARD I.

⑤

NEW
BRUNSWICK

NOVA SCOTIA

Halifax

Québec

MAINE

ATLANTIC

Montréal

Ottawa

St Lawrence Seaway

VERMONT

NEW HAMPSHIRE

MASS.

Boston

Providence

Hartford

CONN.

OCEAN

40

L. Ontario

Rochester

NEW YORK

L Erie

Ⓛ

90

70

Ⓜ

60

Ⓝ

1:12.5M

BRITISH

COLUMBIA

Vancouver
Island

Vancouver

Seattle
Mt Ranier
4392
Spokane

WASHINGTON

Portland

OREGON

CASCADE RANGES

Mt Shasta
4316

San Francisco
San Jose

Reno
Sacramento

CALIFORNIA

SIERRA NEVADA

Mt Whitney
4418
Death Valley

Las
Vegas

Los Angeles

San Bernardino

San Diego

BAJA CALIFORNIA

Coast Ranges

PACIFIC
OCEAN

Golfo de California

Hermosillo

ALBERTA

ROCKY

Edmonton

Calgary

MONTANA

IDAHO

Boise

Great
Salt L.
Salt Lake City

NEVADA

UTAH

UNITED

Grand Canyon

Colorado

ARIZONA

Phoenix

Tucson

MOUNTAINS

WYOMING

COLORADO

Denver

Colorado
Springs

NEW MEXICO

Albuquerque

El Paso

Rio Bravo del Norte

SIERRA MADRE OCCIDENTAL

Chihuahua

Durango

Mazatlán

MEXICO

SASKATCHEWAN

Saskatoon

Regina

Billings

Missouri

Cheyenne

NEBRASKA

KANSAS

Wichita

OKLAHOMA

Oklahoma
City

Amarillo

Lubbock

TEXAS

Colorado

San Antonio

Rio Grande

Monterrey

SIERRA MADRE ORIENTAL

MANIT

A

N

Lake
Winnip

Win

NORTH DAKOTA

Bismarck

SOUTH DAKOTA

Missouri

Lincoln

D

50

100

200

300

400

500

100

200

300 miles

50

120

110

100

130

40

30

120

110

100

① ② ③ ④

Ⓐ Ⓑ Ⓒ

ONTARIO

QUEBEC

James
Bay

Gulf of
Saint Lawrence

Kapuskasing

St. Lawrence

PRINCE
EDWARD I.

Québec

NEW
BRUNSWICK

Fredericton
Saint John

NOVA SCOTIA

Halifax

Thunder
Bay

LAKE SUPERIOR

MICHIGAN

Sudbury

North
Bay

Ottawa

Montréal

St. Lawrence Seaway

MAINE

Augusta

Duluth

LAKE
HURON

Montpelier

NEW HAMPSHIRE

Concord

SOTA

St Paul

WISCONSIN

L. MICHIGAN

Toronto

L. ONTARIO

NEW YORK

VERMONT

Albany

MASS.

Boston

apolis

Mississippi

Niagara
Falls

Buffalo

Hartford

Providence

CONN.

R.I.

Milwaukee

Detroit

LAKE ERIE

Cleveland

MOUNTAINS

Newark

New York

WA

Chicago

Toledo

PENNSYLVANIA

N.J.

Philadelphia

INDIANA

OHIO

Pittsburgh

ILLINOIS

Columbus

Baltimore

MD

Dover

ansas
City

Missouri

St Louis

MISSOURI

Indianapolis

Cincinnati

Ohio

Washington D.C.

Annapolis

DEL.

WEST
Charleston

Louisville

VIRGINIA

VIRGINIA

Richmond

Lexington

Ohio

KENTUCKY

APPALACHIAN

Plateau

ark

Nashville

TENNESSEE

Raleigh

NORTH CAROLINA

Memphis

Columbia

SOUTH
CAROLINA

Little
Rock

ARKANSAS

Atlanta

Birmingham

ATLANTIC

OCEAN

MISSISSIPPI

ALABAMA

GEORGIA

Jackson

Mississippi

LOUISIANA

Baton
Rouge

New Orleans

ston

F

L

Tallahassee

Jacksonville

O

R

Tampa

Lake
Okeechobee

D

A

Miami

Nassau

THE

BAHAMAS

Tropic of Cancer

GULF OF MEXICO

Andros

Straits of Florida

Havana
(Habana)

CUBA

1:15M

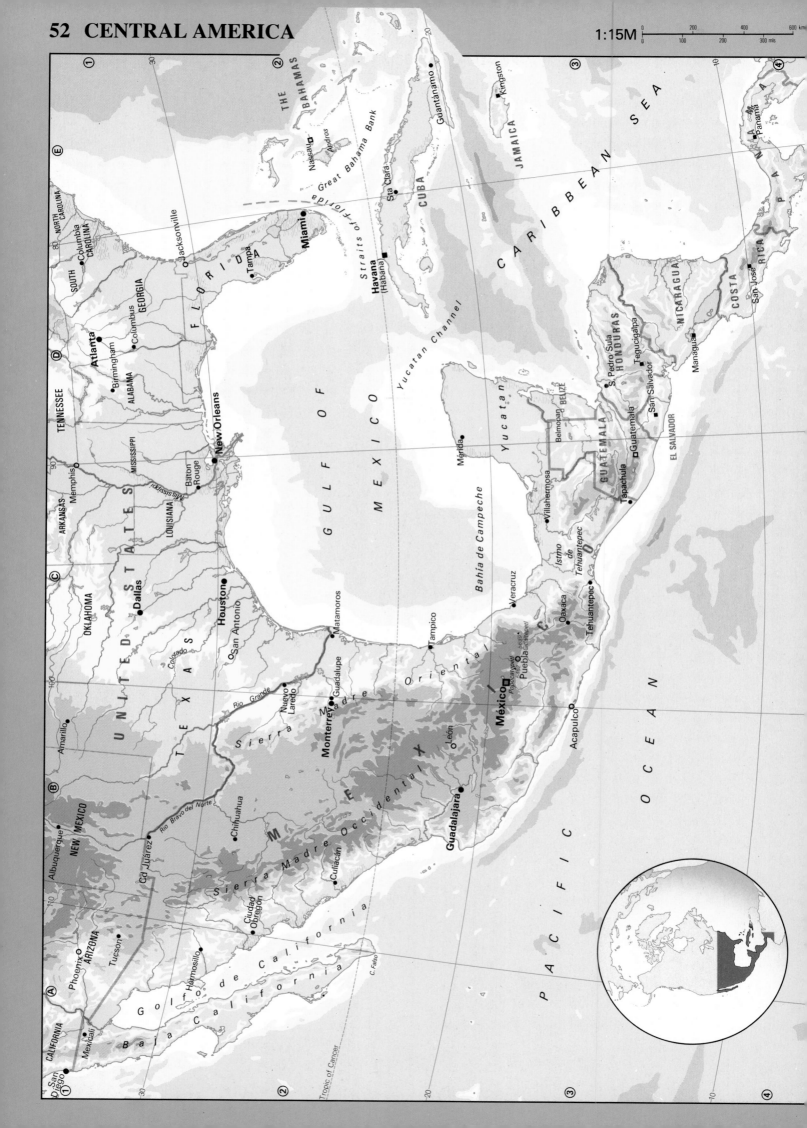

① 30 ② ③ 70 ④

THE BAHAMAS

Nassau□ Andros Great Bahama Bank

Sta Clara

Guantánamo Kingston

CUBA JAMAICA

CARIBBEAN SEA

Straits of Florida

Jacksonville

FLORIDA

Tampa

Miami●

Havana (Habana)■

Yucatán Channel

NORTH CAROLINA

SOUTH CAROLINA Columbia

GEORGIA Atlanta● Columbus

Birmingham ALABAMA

TENNESSEE

UNITED STATES

Memphis○

ARKANSAS

MISSISSIPPI New Orleans●

Baton○ Rouge

LOUISIANA

GULF OF MEXICO

Yucatán

Mérida●

Belmopan BELIZE

GUATEMALA

S. Pedro Sula ● HONDURAS

Tegucigalpa■

San Salvador■

Guatemala□ NICARAGUA

EL SALVADOR Managua■

COSTA RICA

San José●

Panamá

OKLAHOMA

Dallas●

Houston●

San Antonio○

TEXAS

Colorado

Tampico●

Bahía de Campeche

Veracruz●

Istmo de Tehuantepec

Matamoros

Rio Grande

Nuevo Laredo

Guadalupe

Sierra Madre Oriental

Monterrey●

NEW MEXICO

Albuquerque●

Cd Juárez○

Chihuahua●

Rio Bravo del Norte

Sierra Madre Occidental

Culiacán●

León○

Popocatépetl Ixtaccíhuatl Puebla●Citlaltépetl

México□

Oaxaca●

Tehuantepec●

Acapulco○

MÉXICO

Guadalajara●

ARIZONA

Phoenix○

Tucson●

Amarillo●

Ciudad Obregón●

Hermosillo●

Golfo de California

Baja California

C. Falso

Tropic of Cancer

PACIFIC OCEAN

CALIFORNIA

San Diego○

Mexicali●

① ② ③ ④

200 400 600 km
100 200 300 mls

100 200 300 400 km
100 200 mils

Inset maps (scale panels):

Q — 1:25M
DOMINICA
Marigot
Roseau
15°30'
61°30'

R — 1:25M
BARBADOS
Speightstown
Bridgetown
59°30' 13°15'

P — 1:25M
ST LUCIA
Castries
Vieux Fort
14'
61'

N — 1:25M
ST VINCENT
Georgetown
Kingstown
13°15'
61°15'

M — 1:25M
GRENADA
Sauteurs
St George's
12'
61°45'

1:25M
JAMAICA
St Joseph
Arima
Pt of Spain
San Fernando
Fullarton
Gulf of Paria
62
Crown Pt
Moriah
St Joseph
11°15'

Main map labels:

Pt Antonio
Blue Mts
Kingston
Chapeltown
Portland Pt
Mandeville
Savanna la Mar
JAMAICA

ATLANTIC OCEAN

Windward Islands
Leeward Islands
LESSER ANTILLES
Lesser Antilles

ANTIGUA & BARBUDA
Guadeloupe (Fr.)
Basse Terre
DOMINICA
Roseau
Martinique (Fr.)
ST LUCIA
Castries
ST VINCENT
Kingstown
BARBADOS
Bridgetown
GRENADA
St George's

ST KITTS & NEVIS
Virgin Is (U.S.A. & U.K.)

Tobago
TRINIDAD AND TOBAGO
Port of Spain
Trinidad
Carupano
Maturin
Cd Guayana

VENEZUELA
Caracas
Valencia
Barquisimeto
Cabimas
Maracaibo
Valledupar
Ciénaga
G. de Venezuela
Lago de Maracaibo

Barranquilla
Cartagena
Montería
COLOMBIA

PUERTO RICO (U.S.A)
San Juan
Caguas
Ponce
Aguadilla

PUERTO RICO TRENCH

Hispaniola
Santiago
DOMINICAN REPUBLIC
Santo Domingo
Cordillera Central
La Romana
Port-de-Paix
Port-au-Prince
Jacmel
HAITI

THE BAHAMAS
Great Abaco
Eleuthera
Nassau
Andros
Great Inagua
Acklins
Caicos Is (U.K.)

CUBA
Pinar del Rio
Havana (Hábana)
Santa Clara
Sagua la Grande
Camagüey
Holguín
Santiago de Cuba
Montego Bay
Kingston
JAMAICA
Guantánamo

GREATER ANTILLES

CAYMAN TRENCH
Cayman Islands (U.K.)

CARIBBEAN SEA

FLORIDA
Miami
Straits of Florida
Tropic of Cancer

HONDURAS
Caratasca
Prinzapolca
NICARAGUA
COSTA RICA
San José
PANAMA
Panamá
Panama Canal
Golfo del Darién

Gulf of Venezuela

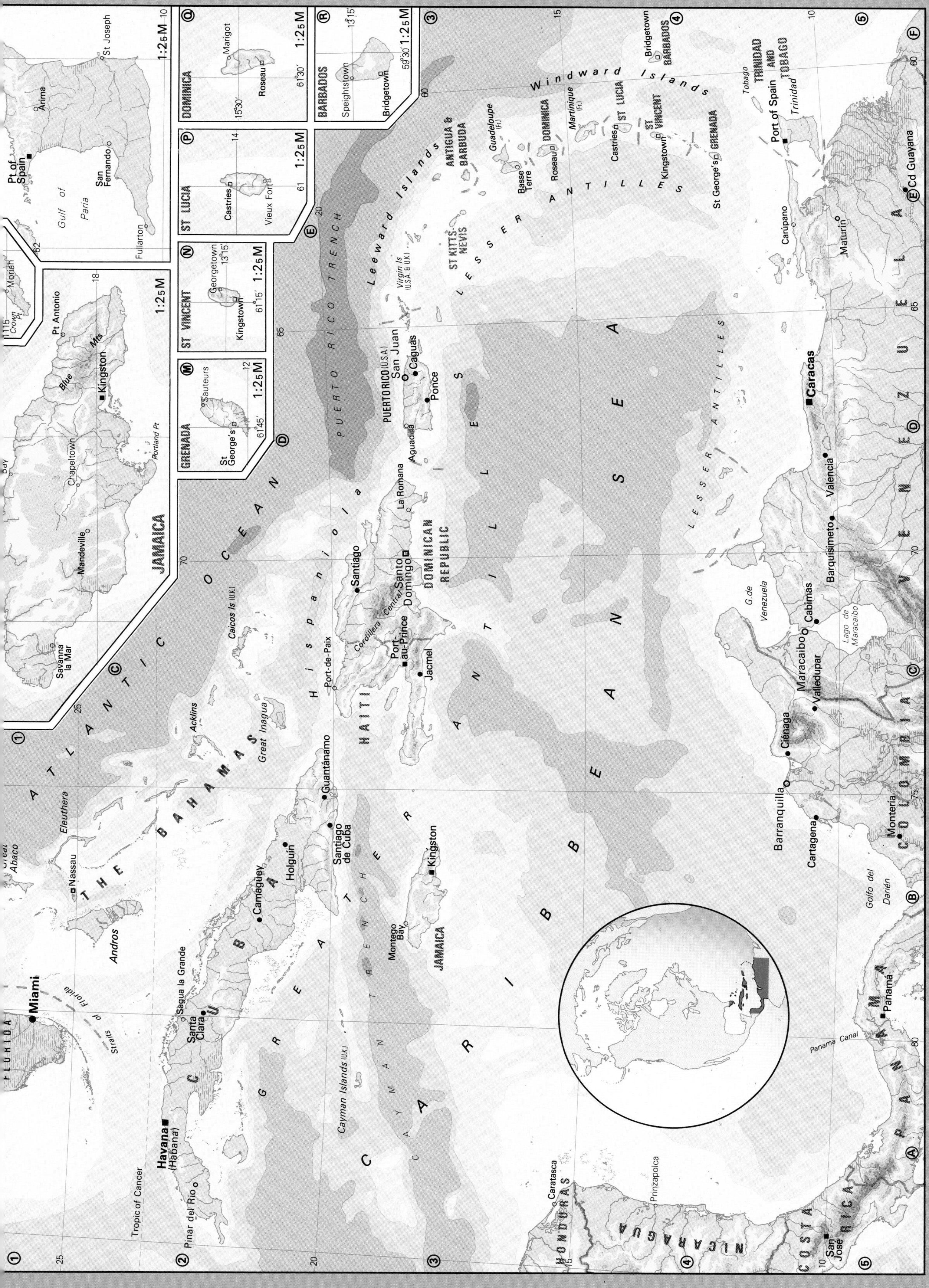

1:35M

250 500 750 1000 km
250 500 mls

A 90 **B** U.S.A. 80 **C** 70 **D** 60 **E** 50 **F** 40 **G**

① Gulf of Mexico
Miami

Tropic of Cancer

THE BAHAMAS

Habana ■

Mérida

CUBA

② MEXICO

BELIZE
Belmopan

GUATEMALA
Guatemala
HONDURAS
Tegucigalpa
S.Salvador
EL SALVADOR
NICARAGUA
Managua

Guantanamo

HAITI
Port au Prince

JAMAICA
Kingston

DOMINICAN REP.
Sto Domingo

Pto Rico (U.S.A.)

Guadaloupe (Fr.)
DOMINICA
Martinique (Fr.)
ST LUCIA
BARBADOS

CARIBBEAN SEA

COSTA RICA
S.José

PANAMA
Panamá

I. del Coco (C.R.)

Malpelo (Col.)

③ Barranquilla
Sta Marta
Maracaibo
Caracas ■
Barcelona
TRINIDAD & TOBAGO

S.Cristóbal
Medellín
VENEZUELA
Cd Bolivar
①
GUYANA
Georgetown
Buenaventura
Bogotá ■
Paramaribo
Cayenne
Cali
Popayán
COLOMBIA
SURINAM
FR. GUIANA
Boa Vista

Orinoco

S.Lorenzo

I. de Marajó

Galapagos Is (Ecu.)
Quito
ECUADOR
Santarem
Equator
S.Pedr
S.Pedr (Bra)

Guayaquil
Negro
Manaus
Belém

SOUTH PACIFIC OCEAN
Iquitos
Amazonas
São Luís
Fortaleza
I. Fernando de Noronha (Braz.)

Purus
Teresina
Natal

④ Trujillo
PERU
Madeira
Tapajós
Xingu
Recife

Pto Velho
②
BRAZIL
Maceió

Callao
Lima
Huancayo
③ Pto Maldonado
Cuzco
Arequipa
La Paz
Cuiabá
Brasília
Goiâna
São Francisco
Salvador

④ BOLIVIA
Cochabamba
Sucre
Sta Cruz
SOUTH ATLANTIC OCEAN

Arica
Corumbá
Belo Horizonte

⑤
Campo Grande
Ribeirão Prêto
Campos
Rio de Janeiro

Antofagasta
PARAGUAY
Paraná
São Paulo
Santos
Trinidade (Braz.)

CHILE
Salta
Asunción
Curitiba
Tropic of Capricorn

S.Miguel de Tucumán
Resistencia
Posadas

Córdoba
Pto Alegre
Santa Fe
Paraná
Pelotas

Mendoza
Rosario
URUGUAY

Valparaíso
Santiago
ARGENTINA
Buenos Aires ■
Montevideo
R.de la Plata

Concepción
Mar del Plata
Bahía Blanca

Valdivia

Pto Montt

Cmd. Rivadavia
G.San Jorge

Falkland Is (U.K.)
Stanley

Rio Gallegos

Punta Arenas
Tierra del Fuego

S.Georgia (U.K.)

S.Shetland Is (U.K.)
S.Orkney Is (U.K.)
S.Sandwich Is (U.K.)

⑥ ANTARCTICA

NORTH AMERICA
AFRICA
SOUTH AMERICA
Pacific Ocean
Atlantic Ocean

④ Reed boat, Lake Titicaca, Bolivia

③ Inca city of Machu-Picchu, Peru

⑥ Emperor penguins in the Antarctic

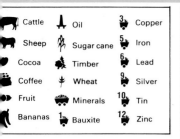

Cattle		Oil		**3**	Copper	
Sheep		Sugar cane		**5**	Iron	
Cocoa		Timber		**6**	Lead	
Coffee		Wheat		**9**	Silver	
Fruit		Minerals		**10**	Tin	
Bananas		Bauxite		**12**	Zinc	

DID YOU KNOW THAT …?

The Angel Falls, Venezuela, are the highest waterfalls in the world, at 979 m (3212 feet).

Deforestation is a major problem in South America. About [per] cent of the total area of forest [is] lost each year! Often trees are [cut] down to clear land for agricul-[tur]e. On hillsides, the soil soon [be]comes too poor to grow crops [and] the land is abandoned. Trees [can]not grow again, and so soil is [erod]ed away by rain and wind. [Tr]ees are also lost when lakes are [ma]de for hydro-electric dams; [wh]en new towns are built; and as a [res]ult of the way people live – they [us]e too much wood for fuel and [tim]ber, allow animals to graze on [foli]age, and light fires which get [ou]t of control.

In the Andes Mountains, in the north-west of South America, [the]re are ruins of cities built by the [Inc]as. They ruled the Indians in the [are]a 500 years ago. The Incas had [wel]l-developed political and reli-[gio]us systems. They built their [cit]ies on terraces engineered from [the] mountain side. The Spanish, [the] first Europeans to discover [the]se cities, killed the Incas to seize [the] gold and silver which they had [ow]ned, and their cities were aban-[do]ned.

The highest navigable lake in the world is Lake Titicaca, on [the] Peru/Bolivia border. It is no [les]s than 3811 m (12 503 feet) [ab]ove sea level! The local Indian [peo]ple make boats from bundles of [ree]ds tied together, to use for [fis]hing. The reeds grow around the [ed]ge of the lake.

Although in the rain forests of the Amazon Basin it rains ev-[er]y day, in the Atacama Desert, [Ch]ile, hundreds of years can pass [bet]ween one rain storm and the [ne]xt! A storm in 1971 was the first [for] 400 years. The desert is the [dri]est place in the world.

The Emperor Penguin, found [in] the Antarctic, does not [ma]ke a nest. Instead, a single egg is [car]ried on top of the male pen-[gu]in's feet! It is kept warm by a [fol]d of skin which hangs down and [co]vers it. The penguin does not eat [du]ring the two months it takes for [th]e egg to hatch out!

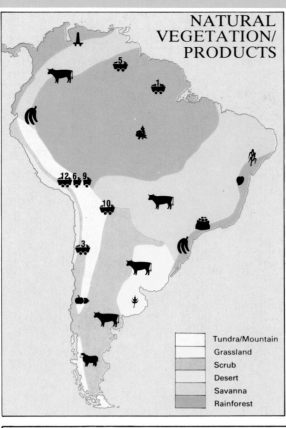

NATURAL VEGETATION/PRODUCTS

Tundra/Mountain
Grassland
Scrub
Desert
Savanna
Rainforest

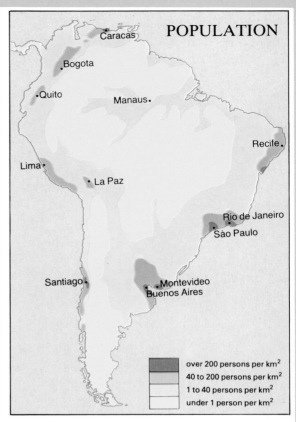

POPULATION

Caracas
Bogota
Quito
Manaus
Lima
La Paz
Recife
Rio de Janeiro
São Paulo
Santiago
Montevideo
Buenos Aires

over 200 persons per km²
40 to 200 persons per km²
1 to 40 persons per km²
under 1 person per km²

ARGENTINA

Area: 2 777 815 sq km
(1 072 514 sq miles)
Population: 29 100 000
Capital: Buenos Aires
Language: Spanish
Currency: Argentine Peso

BOLIVIA

Area: 1 098 575 sq km
(424 160 sq miles)
Population: 6 000 000
Capital: La Paz
Languages: Spanish,
Aymara, Quechua
Currency: Bolivian Peso

BRAZIL

Area: 8 511 968 sq km
(3 286 471 sq miles)
Population: 134 400 000
Capital: Brasilia
Language: Portuguese
Currency: Cruzeiro

CHILE

Area: 756 943 sq km
(292 256 sq miles)
Population: 11 900 000
Capital: Santiago
Language: Spanish
Currency: Chilean Peso

COLOMBIA

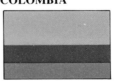

Area: 1 138 907 sq km
(439 732 sq miles)
Population: 28 200 000
Capital: Bogota
Language: Spanish
Currency: Colombian Peso

ECUADOR

Area: 455 502 sq km
(175 869 sq miles)
Population: 9 100 000
Capital: Quito
Language: Spanish
Currency: Sucre

GUYANA

Area: 214 969 sq km
(83 000 sq miles)
Population: 800 000
Capital: Georgetown
Language: English
Currency: Guyanese Dollar

PERU

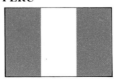

Area: 1 285 215 sq km
(496 222 sq miles)
Population: 19 200 000
Capital: Lima
Languages: Spanish,
Aymara, Quechua
Currency: Sol

VENEZUELA

Area: 912 047 sq km
(352 141 sq miles)
Population: 18 600 000
Capital: Caracas
Language: Spanish
Currency: Bolivar

1:15M

Roseau
Martinique
ST LUCIA
Castries
ST VINCENT
Kingstown
GRENADA
St Ge

Ⓐ   85   Ⓑ   80   Ⓒ   75   Ⓓ   70   Ⓔ   65

Tegucigalpa

Neth. Antilles
Curaçao
(Neth.)

① Managua

NICARAGUA

Sta Marta

Maracaibo   Caracas
Cabimas

Valencia   Maracay
Barranquilla   Barquisimeto
Valledupar

Orinoco   Cd Guaya

10   Panamá
Panamá   Monteria
PANAMA
Cúcuta
COSTA RICA   San José   San Cristóbal
VENEZUELA
Bucaramanga

L   L   A   N   O   S

②   Bello   Orinoco
Itagui   Medellín   Angel
Manizales   Falls

Pereira   Armenia   Bogotá
Cartago
Buenaventura   Orinoco
5   Palmira   RORAI
Cali   COLOMBIA
Neiva

Calamar

③   Pasto   Içana

Negro

Quito   5896
Cotopaxi
0   ECUADOR   Manacap
Chimborazo
5267
Guayaquil   A   M   A   Z   O   N
Iquitos   Amazonas
④   Tabatinga
S   E   L   V   A   S
Piura   Humaitá
5   Cruzeiro do Sul
Chiclayo   A   C   R   E
Pôrto Velho
Trujillo   Pucallpa
⑤   Chimbote   Rio Branco   RONDÔNI
C   O   R   D   I   L   L   E   R   A

B
PERU
10   Callao   Huancayo
Lima   Machu Picchu
Cuzco   Trinidad
⑥   D   E
L   O   S
A   N   D   E   S   Ancohuma
6388
Titicaca
15   Arequipa   La Paz   BOLIVI
Cochabamba
Santa Cruz
Oruro
⑦   Arica

P   A   C   I   F   I   C

O   C   E   A   N

Jujuy

90   Ⓐ   85

95   90   at the same scale

CHILE
20
Tropic of Capricorn
Antofagasta
ARGENTINA
GALAPAGOS ISLANDS   at the same scale   Salta
(ISLAS GALÁPAGOS)   Islas Juan Fernández
(Chile)
Isabela   Santa Cruz   Alejandro Selkirk   Robinson Crusoe
Baquerizo   Sta Clara
Moreno
Ⓝ   90   Ⓠ   35   Ⓓ   70   Ⓔ   Ⓕ

BADOS
getown

AD
GO

 uma

G

55   H   50   J   45   K   40   L   35   M   15

①

A T L A N T I C

10

Georgetown

ANA   SURINAM   FRENCH
Paramaribo   GUIANA

O C E A N

②

Cayenne

⑤

AMAPÁ

Macapá

Equator

0

Amazonas

Santarém   Belém

Cametá

São Luís

Monçãoo

Itaituba   P A R Á   MARANHÃO

Sobral   Fortaleza (Ceará)   ④

Imperatriz   Teresina

C E A R Á   Mossoró

RIO GRANDE DO NORTE   Natal   5

Serra do Cachimbo   Araguaina   P I A U Í   PARAÍBA   João Pessoa

R   PERNAMBUCO   Caruaru   Recife (Pernambuco)   ⑤

São Francisco

A   ALAGOAS   Maceió

São Félix   Z   SERGIPE   10

B A H I A   Aracajú

MATO GROSSO   Barreiras   Feira de S.

I

GOIÁS   Salvador (Bahia)   ⑥

Planalto de   Jequié

Paraná   Vitória da
Mato Grosso   Conquista   Ilhéus

Cáceres   Brasília   São Francisco   Serra do Espinhaço

Goiânia   Montes Claros   15

Itamaraju

Teófilo Otôni

Uberlândia   M I N A S   G E R A I S   ESPÍRITO

MATO GROSSO   Uberaba   Colatina
DO SUL   Belo   Caratinga   SANTO   ⑦

Campo Grande   Horizonte

Franca   Cachoeiro

Dourados   S Ã O   P A U L O   20

Pres. Prudente   Marília   Volta   Nova Friburgo
Limeria   Redonda

Londrina   Sa de Mantiqueira

Umuarama   Sorocaba   São Vicente   ⑧

ARAGUAY   Toledo P A R A N Á   São Paulo   Rio
de Janeiro

Asunción   55   J   45   K   40   L   35   M   30

1:15M

0   200   400   600 km
0 100   200   300 mls

B O L I V I A

B R A Z I L

MATO GROSSO
DO SUL

MINAS
GERAIS

Belo
Horizon

Arica
Oruro
Santa
Cruz

Potosí

Campo Grande

S. José
do R. Prêto

Franca

Tropic of Capricorn
Antofagasta

Jujuy
Orán

Tarija

Dourados

SÃO   PAULO

Limeria
Sa.de Mantiqu

P A R A G U A Y

Umuarama

São
Paulo

Rio
Jan

Salta

Asunción

Toledop A R A N A

Londrina

Itapeva

Desierto de Atacama

Catamarca

S.Miguel de
Tucumán

Chaco

Guarapuava

Curitiba

Copiapó

GRAN CHACO

Santiago
del
Estero

Resistencia

Corrientes

SANTA CATARINA

Joinville

La Rioja

Salinas Grandes

Paraná

Corrientes

Uruguay

Passo Fundo

Florianópolis

Coquimbo

San Juan

Córdoba

Santa
Fe

RIO GRANDE

S.Juan

Aconcagua
6960

Mendoza

San   Córdoba

Paraná

DO SUL

Bagé

Pôrto Alegre

Valparaíso

ANDES

Santiago

Luis

Santa Fe
Paraná

U R U G U A Y

Rio Grande

Rancagua

Rosario

Alegrete

LOS

CORDILLERA   DE

Mendoza

A R G E N T I N A

PAMPAS

Buenos
Aires

Florida

Buenos
Aires

La Plata

Montevideo

Concepción

La   Pampa

Neuquén

Mar del Plata

Temuco

Bahía Blanca

Río
Negro

Osorno

Maquinchao

Golfo
San Matías

A T L A N T I C

Puerto Montt

Trelew

CORDILLERA

Chubut

O C E A N

Archipiélago
de las
Chones

PATAGONIA

Coihaique

Comodoro Rivadavia

Santa   Cruz

S. Julián

FALKLAND ISLANDS
(ISLAS MALVINAS)
(U.K.)

Río Gallegos

Stanley

Arch. de la
Reina Adelaida

Est. de Magallanes

Punta Arenas

Tierra del Fuego

Cape Horn

South Geo
(U.K.)

This index helps you to find countries and places shown on the maps in this atlas. Each country or place name is listed in alphabetical order (A to Z), letter by letter. For example, Manchester will come after Madagascar and before Melbourne. After each name, extra information in a shortened form may be given. For example, 'Mts' after the entry 'Grampian' means 'mountains'. The list of abbreviations (shortened words) which follows this introduction tells you what each shortened word description means. The next item in each entry is the name of the country in which the place is. Finally there is a reference number which will look something like this: 16C3. The first number (before the letter) is the page number (here page 16). The letter and second number lead you to the area on the map on that page where the place can be found. Follow the column labelled with the letter shown (here column C) down from the top of the page. Follow the row with the same number (here row 3) in from the side of the page. Where the column and row meet is the part of the map where you will find the place you looked up (16C3 is the reference for London, England). Practise looking up a few places in the index and on the maps. Try to find Sydney, Australia; New York, U.S.A.; Paris, France.

Arch	Archipelago	O	Ocean
B	Bay	P	Pass
C	Cape	Pass	Passage
Chan	Channel	Pen	Peninsula
Des	Desert	Plat	Plateau
Gl	Glacier	Pt	Point
G. of	Gulf of	Res	Reservoir
H(s)	Hills(s)	R	River
I(s)	Islands(s)	S	Sea
Lg	Lagoon	Sd	Sound
L	Lake	Str	Strait
Mt(s)	Mountain(s)	V	Valley

A

Abādān *Iran*	41A4
Abéché *Chad*	24C2
Aberdeen *Scotland*	16C2
Abidjan *Ivory Coast*	23B4
Abū Dhabi *U.A.E.*	38P3
Acapulco *Mexico*	52C3
Accra *Ghana*	23B4
Acklins, I *Caribbean*	53C2
Aconcagua, Mt *Chile*	58B4
Acre, State *Brazil*	56D5
Addis Ababa *Ethiopia*	24D3
Adelaide *Australia*	42C4
Aden = ('Adan) *S. Yemen*	38C4
Aden, G. of *Yemen/Somalia*	38C4
Adriatic, Sea *Italy/Yugos*	18C2
Afghanistan, Republic *Asia*	26E4
Āgra *India*	39F3
Aguadilla *Puerto Rico*	53D3
Ahmadābād *India*	39F3
Ahvāz *Iran*	41E3
Ajaccio *Corsica*	18B2
Akita *Japan*	37E4
Aktyubinsk *USSR*	32G4
Akureyri *Iceland*	13B1
Alabama, State *USA*	51E3
Alagoas, State *Brazil*	57L5
Alaska, G. of *USA*	48D4
Alaska, State *USA*	48C3
Alaska Range, Mts *USA*	48C3
Albacete *Spain*	20B2
Albania, Republic *Europe*	11H4
Albany *USA*	51F2
Alberta, Province *Canada*	48G4
Alborg *Denmark*	14B1
Al Bū Kamāl *Syria*	41D3
Albuquerque *USA*	50C3
Alegrete *Brazil*	58E3
Aleutian Range, Mts *USA*	48C4
Alexandria *Egypt*	41A3
Algeria, Republic *N. Africa*	21E5
Algiers = (Alger) *Algeria*	20C2
Al Hadithah *Iraq*	41D3
Al Hudaydah *Yemen*	24E2
Alicante *Spain*	20B2
Alice Springs *Australia*	42C3
Al'Īsawiyah *Saudi Arabia*	41C3
Al Jālāmid *Saudi Arabia*	41D3
Al Lādhiqīyah *Syria*	41C2
Allāhābād *India*	39G3
Alma-Ata *USSR*	39F1
Al Manāmah *Bahrain*	38D3
Al Mudawwara *Jordan*	41C4
Alpi Dolomitiche, Mts *Italy*	18C1
Alps, Mts *Europe*	18B1
Altai, Mts *Mongolia*	32K5
Altay, Mts *USSR*	32K4
Amapá, State *Brazil*	57H3
Amarillo *USA*	50C3
Amazonas, R *Brazil*	57H4
Amazonas, State *Brazil*	56E4
Ambarchik *USSR*	45C7
Ambon *Indonesia*	42B1
American Samoa, Is *Pacific O.*	43H2
Amery Ice Shelf *Antarctica*	45G10
Amman *Jordan*	41C3
Amsterdam *Netherlands*	14A2
Amundsen, S *Antarctica*	45F4
Amur, R *USSR*	33P4
Anchorage *USA*	48D3
Ancohuma, Mt *Bolivia*	56E7
Ancona *Italy*	18C2
Andorra, Principality *S.W. Europe*	20C1
Andorra-La-Vella *Andorra*	20C1
Angmagssalik *Greenland*	49P3
Angola, Republic *Africa*	21F9
Ankara *Turkey*	41B2
'Annaba *Algeria*	23C1
An Najaf *Iraq*	41D3
Annapolis *USA*	51F3
An Nāsirīyah *Iraq*	41E3
Anshan *China*	36E1
Antananarivo *Madagascar*	25E5
Antarctic, Pen *Antarctica*	45G3
Antarctic Circle *Antarctica*	45G1
Antigua and Barbuda, Is *Caribbean*	53E3
Antofagasta *Chile*	58B2
Antwerp *Belgium*	17C1
Apia *W. Samoa*	43H2
Appalachian, Mts *USA*	51E3
Appennines, Mts *Italy*	18C2
Arabian, S *Asia/Arabian Peninsula*	38E4
Arad *Romania*	15E3
Arafura, S *Indonesia/Australia*	42D1
Araguaína *Brazil*	57J5
Arbīl *Iraq*	41D2
Arctic Circle	45C1
Arctic, Ocean *N. Europe*	32
Ardabīl *Iran*	41E2
Argentina, Republic *S. America*	54D7
Århus *Denmark*	13G7
Arica *Chile*	58B1
Arizona, State *USA*	50B3
Arkansas, State *USA*	51D3

Arkhangel'sk *USSR*	32F3
Armenia *Colombia*	56C3
Ar Rutbah *Iraq*	41D3
Asahikawa *Japan*	37E3
Ashkhabad *USSR*	38D2
Asmara *Ethiopia*	24D2
Astrakhan' *USSR*	32F5
Asunción *Paraguay*	58E3
Aswân *Egypt*	38B3
Atbara *Sudan*	24D2
Athabasca, L *Canada*	48H4
Athens = (Athinai) *Greece*	19E3
Atlanta *USA*	51E3
Atlantic, O	10C3
Auckland *New Zealand*	44B1
Augusta *USA*	51G2
Australia, Commonwealth Nation *S.W. Pacific*	27H7
Austria, Federal Republic *Europe*	10G4
Ayers Rock *Australia*	42C3
Azores, Islands *Atlantic O.*	23A1

B

Badajoz *Spain*	20A2
Baden-Württemburg, State *W. Germany*	14B3
Baffin, B *Greenland/Canada*	49M2
Baffin, I *Canada*	49L3
Bagé *Brazil*	58F4
Baghdād *Iraq*	41D3
Bahamas, The, Is *Caribbean*	51F4
Bahia, State *Brazil*	57K6
Bahía Blanca *Argentina*	58D5
Bahia de Campeche, B *Mexico*	52C2
Bahrain, Sheikdom *Arabian Peninsula*	38D3
Baja California, State *Mexico*	50B4
Baku *USSR*	32F5
Balearic, Is *Spain*	20C2
Balikpapan *Indonesia*	42A1
Baltic, S *N. Europe*	13H7
Baltimore *USA*	51F3
Bamako *Mali*	23B3
Banda Aceh *Indonesia*	40B4
Bandung *Indonesia*	35D7
Bangalore *India*	39F4
Bangassou *C.A.R.*	24C3
Bangkok *Thailand*	40C3
Bangladesh, Republic *Asia*	26F4
Bangui *C.A.R.*	24B3
Ban Hat Yai *Thailand*	40C4
Banjarmasin *Indonesia*	35E7
Banjul *The Gambia*	23A3
Banks, I *Canada*	48F2
Ban Me Thuot *Vietnam*	40D3
Baotou *China*	36C1
Barbados, I *Caribbean*	53F4
Barcelona *Spain*	20C1
Barents, S *USSR*	32D2
Bari *Italy*	18D2
Barnaul *USSR*	32K4
Barquisimeto *Venezuela*	56E1
Barranquilla *Colombia*	56D1
Basel *Switzerland*	18B1
Basra *Iraq*	41E3
Basse Terre *Guadeloupe*	53E3
Bass Strait *Australia*	42D4
Bata *Equat. Guinea*	24A3
Batna *Algeria*	23C1
Batumi *USSR*	41D1
Beaufort, S *Canada*	45B5
Béchar *Algeria*	23B1
Beersheba *Israel*	41B3
Beirut *Lebanon*	41C3
Belém *Brazil*	57J4
Belfast *N. Ireland*	16B3
Belgium, Kingdom *N.W. Europe*	10F3
Belgrade = (Beograd) *Yugoslavia*	19E2
Belize, Republic *C. America*	52D3
Bellingshausen, S *Antarctica*	45G3
Bello *Colombia*	56C2
Belo Horizonte *Brazil*	57K7
Beloye More, S *USSR*	32E3
Bengal, B. of *Asia*	39G4
Benin, Republic *Africa*	21E7

Benin City *Nigeria*	23C4
Benxi *China*	36E1
Berbera *Somalia*	24E2
Bergen *Norway*	13F6
Bering, S *USSR/USA*	33T3
Bering, Str *USSR/USA*	45C6
Berlin *Germany*	14C2
Bern *Switzerland*	18B1
Bhutan, Kingdom *Asia*	26F4
Bialystok *Poland*	15E2
Bight of Benin, B *W. Africa*	23C4
Bight of Biafra, B *Cameroon*	23C4
Bilbao *Spain*	20B1
Billings *USA*	50C2
Birmingham *England*	16C3
Birmingham *USA*	51E3
Bir Moghrein *Mauritania*	23A2
Biscay, B *France/Spain*	17A2
Bissau *Guinea Bissau*	23A3
Black, S *USSR/Europe*	32E5
Black Volta, R *Burkina*	23B3
Blagoveshchensk *USSR*	33O4
Blanc, Mt *France/Italy*	17D2
Blantyre *Malawi*	25D5
Bloemfontein *S. Africa*	25C6
Blue, Mts *Jamaica*	53J1
Bobo Dioulasso *Burkina*	23B3
Bobruysk *USSR*	15F2
Bodø *Norway*	13G5
Bogotá *Colombia*	56D3
Boise *USA*	50B2
Bolgatanga *Ghana*	23B3
Bolivia, Republic *S. America*	54D5
Bologna *Italy*	17E3
Bombay *India*	39F4
Bonn *W. Germany*	14B2
Bordeaux *France*	17B3
Borneo, I *Malaysia/Indonesia*	35E6
Bornholm, I *Denmark*	13G7
Bosporus, Sd *Turkey*	19F2
Boston *USA*	51F2
Bothnia, G. of *Sweden/Finland*	13H6
Botswana, Republic *Africa*	21G10
Bouaké *Ivory Coast*	23B4
Boulogne *France*	17C1
Brahmaputra, R *India*	39H3
Brasilia *Brazil*	57J7
Bratsk *USSR*	33M4
Brazil, Republic *S. America*	54E4
Brazzaville *Congo*	24B4
Bremen *W. Germany*	14B2
Brenner, P *Austria/Italy*	14C3
Breslau *Poland*	14D2
Brest *France*	17B2
Bridgetown *Barbados*	53F4
Brisbane *Australia*	43E3
Bristol *England*	16C3
British Columbia, Province *Canada*	48F4
Brooks Range, Mts *USA*	48C3
Brunei, Sultanate *S.E. Asia*	35E6
Brussels = (Brüssel/Bruxelles) *Belgium*	14A2
Bryansk *USSR*	32E4
Bucaramanga *Colombia*	56D2
Bucharest = (Bucureşti) *Romania*	19F2
Budapest *Hungary*	15D3
Buenaventura *Colombia*	56C3
Buenos Aires *Argentina*	58E4
Buenos Aires, State *Argentina*	58E5
Buffalo *USA*	51F2
Bujumbura *Burundi*	24C4
Bukavu *Zaïre*	24C4
Bulawayo *Zimbabwe*	25C6
Bulgaria, Republic *Europe*	11H4
Burgas *Bulgaria*	38A1
Burgos *Spain*	20B1
Burkina, Republic *Africa*	21F8
Burma, Republic *Asia*	26F4
Burundi, Republic *Africa*	21G8

C

Cabimas *Venezuela*	56D1
Cabinda, Province *Angola*	24B4
Cáceres *Brazil*	57G7
Cachoeiro de Itapemirim *Brazil*	57K8